Britain's Black Population

Britain's Black Population

The Runnymede Trust
and
The Radical Statistics Race Group

HEINEMANN EDUCATIONAL BOOKS

Heinemann Educational Books Ltd
22 Bedford Square, London WC1B 3HH

LONDON   EDINBURGH   MELBOURNE   AUCKLAND
HONG KONG   SINGAPORE   KUALA LUMPUR   NEW DELHI
IBADAN   NAIROBI   JOHANNESBURG
EXETER (NH)   KINGSTON   PORT OF SPAIN

British Library Cataloguing in Publication Data

Runnymede Trust.
    Britain's Black population.
    1. Blacks – Great Britain – Social conditions
    I. Title   II. Radical Statistics Race Group
    301.45′19′6041   DA125.N4

    ISBN 0–435–82781–2
    ISBN 0–435–82782–0 Pbk

Printed in Great Britain by
Biddles Ltd, Guildford, Surrey

256,945

B/18297

Contents

The Runnymede Trust

The Runnymede Trust is a registered educational charity which was established in 1968. The main objectives of the Trust are the collection and dissemination of information and the promotion of public education on immigration and race relations. This is done by a number of means:

- An information service which provides accurate and up-to-date information on race relations and immigration;
- A monthly information Bulletin;
- Publications, including pamphlets, occasional studies, and briefing papers, on matters of current concern;
- Seminars and meetings;
- Specialist consultancy work in industry;
- Major census analysis project.

The full list of Runnymede Trust publications and other information concerning race relations and immigration in Britain and in the EEC are available from the Runnymede Trust.

THE RUNNYMEDE TRUST
62 CHANDOS PLACE
LONDON WC2N 4HG

Radical Statistics Race Group

The Radical Statistics Group was formed in January 1975 by statisticians and research workers drawn together by a common concern about the political assumptions and implications of much of their work and of the actual and potential uses of statistics and statistical techniques. Membership of the group is open to all those working in or interested in the field of statistics from a politically radical perspective.

Within the group are sub-groups with special interests either in theoretical questions or in the political implications of applications in specific areas such as education and health. The Race Group was formed in 1978 with the specific aim of producing this book.

For details of publications and activities contact

RADICAL STATISTICS GROUP
c/o BSSRS
9 POLAND STREET
LONDON W1V 3DG

Biographical Notes on the Contributors

The Runnymede Trust

Usha Prashar: Director.
Shān Nicholas: Assistant Director.
Julian Henriques: Information and Research Officer.

Individuals

Katya Lestor: Formerly Assistant Editor of the *Human Rights Review*.
Robert Miles: Lecturer in Sociology at the University of Glasgow. He is the co-editor of *Racism and Political Action in Britain* (Routledge & Kegan Paul, 1979), and co-author of *Labour and Racism* (Routledge & Kegan Paul, 1980).

Radical Statistics Race Group

Heather Booth: Demographer and active member of the Radical Statistics Group. She worked on this book whilst studying for a postgraduate research degree. She now works in the SSRC Research Unit for Ethnic Relations at the University of Aston in Birmingham.

Dave Drew: Senior Lecturer in Statistics at Sheffield City Polytechnic. His main preoccupation during the two years prior to the publication of this book has been co-ordinating the Radstats Race Group. He also has a research interest in population forecasting in multiracial areas.

Mike Grimsley: Senior Lecturer in Social Statistics at Sheffield City Polytechnic and was formerly a research statistician at the Institute of Child Health, University of London.

Peter Long: Senior Lecturer in Operational Research at Sheffield City Polytechnic.

Shanti Patel: Senior Lecturer in Economics at Sheffield City Polytechnic and is particularly interested in the transition from school to work for young black school leavers.

Colin Thunhurst: Senior Lecturer in Mathematics and Statistics for Social Sciences at Sheffield City Polytechnic. He has been an active member of the British Society for Social Responsibility in Science for several years, and a frequent contributor to its journal, *Science for People*.

Nic Wright: Statistician at the Greater London Council working particularly in the social, housing and transportation areas.

Preface

The Runnymede Trust and the Radical Statistics Race Group co-operated in a joint project to produce this book. It has been compiled by a number of people. Chapter 1 has been written by Heather Booth and Dave Drew; chapter 2 by Katya Lester and Usha Prashar; Chapter 3 by Julian Henriques, Peter Long and Shanti Patel; Chapter 4 by Julian Henriques and Nic Wright; Chapter 5 by Mike Grimsley, Shān Nicholas and Colin Thunhurst; Chapter 6 by Shān Nicholas and Chapter 7 by Dave Drew. Robert Miles edited the book. His help was invaluable in drawing together the work of different authors. We would like to thank Alix Henley, Dougal Hutchison, Galen Ives, Warren Gilchrist, Stewart Lansley, David Owen, Ralph Taylor, Cathy Dean and Doug Bell for making constructive criticisms of the draft at various stages. We would like to thank Sue Drew, Jean Harper, Anna DiGiovanna, Christine Dunn, Angela Green, Shirley Harrison, Renee Hayes and Sue Lomas who with patience typed and proof-read the draft. Our special thanks are due to Patricia Oakley who co-ordinated administration for the Runnymede Trust, especially during the final stages.

Introduction

This book has three main aims. The first is to provide a statistical picture of Britain's black population. The second is to describe the official policy responses by local and central government and the third is to discuss the inadequacies of the available statistics and the problems in using them.

The subject matter of the book should be viewed in the context of two major issues. The first is the nature and extent of the active response of black minorities themselves to the discrimination and disadvantage which they face and second, the changing political scene. Concentration on official responses is not intended to suggest that there have been no other responses. Britain's black communities are increasingly organising themselves to respond to the specific problems which they face. Much of this activity often goes unmentioned and unrecognised by government, policymakers and the majority of Britain's population, except when some 'dramatic' events occur. The long industrial dispute at Imperial Typewriters Limited in 1974 and the recent strikes at Grunwick and the Chix Sweet Factory in Slough have demonstrated that black workers are not prepared to accept passively racial discrimination either by employers or by trade unions. Similarly the reaction of the black community in Southall in 1976 to the murder of a young Sikh and in 1979 to the decision of the National Front to hold a meeting in Southall clearly illustrates the strengths of the black community.

Moreover, black minorities' involvement in the day-to-day work of organising weekend and evening language classes, providing training facilities for unemployed black youths, organising single-parent families to demand more assistance from local authorities, fighting decisions of the immigration authorities, organising self-defence groups to protect themselves from racist violence and a whole range of self-help initiatives are equally important and should be borne in mind when reading this book.

The second major issue is the political debate that surrounded and gave rise to the immigration legislation in the 1960s and the continuing debate in the 1970s, a period which has witnessed the emergence of the National Front, greater incidence of overt racism and an increase in political violence against black people; for example, the attacks and fire bombings of black bookshops in 1976 and the physical attacks on Bengalis in the East End of London. In the late 1970s the riots in Lewisham, Ladywood and Notting Hill were poignant reminders of the grave tensions that exist in our inner cities. Relationships between the black communities and police have caused substantial controversy and have become one of the major areas of concern.

Now, a comment about the title of the book and why we have chosen the term 'black population'. What the immigrants from New Commonwealth and Pakistan (NCWP) and their children born have in common is the material consequences and, in very many cases, the direct experience of discrimination. Discrimination, as the studies, by Political and Economic Planning (PEP) have demonstrated, is based upon colour. Hence, the reference to Britain's black population. It can, of course, be argued that some immigrants and their children do not and would not want to be labelled as *black*. That is not denied, but the defence of this terminology in this context lies with the fact that, irrespective of their own particular beliefs, experiences and the wide range of cultural variations, racism and racial discrimination is a crucial determinant of their economic and social situation.

Finally, it should be stated that our intention has been to present in a clear and straightforward manner some basic factual information about Britain's black population, drawing upon statistics and research findings. It could be argued that by writing this book we only increase the preoccupation with numbers. This is certainly not our intention. Rather it is that the statistics should provide a factual framework for a constructive debate. We have tried to fill what is, in some areas, a complete 'statistical vacuum' and, in others, a 'partial vacuum' with many gaps in the information available. The main text has not therefore been overloaded with academic references and diagrams are included to aid the presentation of information. Chapter 1 sketches a statistical profile of the black population. Chapter 2 deals with government responses, mainly legislation, to deal with immigration, racial discrimination and racial disadvantage. Chapters 3, 4, 5, 6 deal with employment, housing, education and health and social services respectively. We have attempted to include relevant information available until December 1979.

For the reader who wishes to follow up certain issues in more detail, a select bibliography of books is provided, together with separate lists of the publications of the Runnymede Trust, the Commission for Racial Equality, the Institute of Race Relations and the SSRC Research Unit on Ethnic Relations. We hope that this book will not only be read by those searching for basic information about the economic and social circumstances of black population in Britain, but also used for more informed discussion of the issues involved.

USHA PRASHAR
Director
Runnymede Trust

DAVE DREW
Radical Statistics
Race Group

Dedicated to Nelson Mandela who is still in prison in South Africa:

'For our own part we wish to make it perfectly clear that we shall never cease to fight against repression and injustice.'

From *No Easy Walk to Freedom* by Nelson Mandela (Heinemann Educational Books, 1973)

1 Britain's Black Population

Chapter 1 comprises background information on the numbers of black people in Britain, where they live and their demographic characteristics (i.e. births, deaths and marriages). Our object is to provide a factual starting-point for discussion of the specific issues of racial discrimination, the material disadvantages of black people, and various official policy responses to discrimination and disadvantage. We begin by presenting statistics on the size of the black population in Britain and not immigration statistics. The political and public debate about the black population usually proceeds from the 'facts' about immigration, but such a starting-point assumes that all black people in Britain are immigrants and that all immigrants to Britain are black. Both assumptions are false as illustrated below.

It should be noted at the outset that difficulties arise in using official statistics because of differences in definitions and inadequacies in the data collected. This means that the terminology used in the text varies. Where possible, only fleeting mention is made of these technical difficulties, which are discussed more fully in Chapter 7.

The size of the black population

The growth in Britain's black population is a postwar phenomenon (see Fig. 1.1). In 1951 there were 1.6 million people living in Britain who were born outside the UK, of whom only 0.2 million were born in the New Commonwealth.[1] By 1971 there were 3.0 million people who were born outside the UK of whom 1.2 million were born in the New Commonwealth. The majority of these 1.2 million were black workers attracted to Britain during the 1950s and 1960s by employment opportunities. For example, London Transport advertised at the time to encourage immigrants from the West Indies to come to Britain.

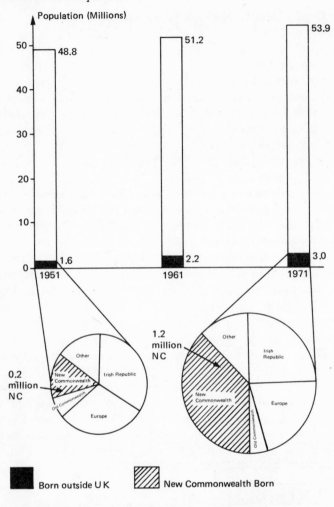

Source: OPCS, *Demographic Review*; London: HMSO, 1977, table 5.7.

Fig. 1.1 Resident population of Great Britain by country of birth.

The source of statistics on population size is the ten-yearly population census. Data have been collected regularly on place of birth but this does not give an accurate indication of the number of black people living in Britain. Taking India as an example, nearly one-third of those enumerated in the 1966 Census as born in India were white (the 'White Indians'), born there during the period of British colonial rule. Despite these difficulties, birthplace data have to be used prior to 1971.

A clearer statistical picture for 1971 is possible as a result of changes in the Census. Information collected for the first time in 1971 about birthplace of parents enables estimates of the population of New Commonwealth 'ethnic origin' to be made which includes black people born in Britain to parents born in the New Commonwealth. (The technical difficulties of this are discussed in Chapter 7. Suffice it to say that neither birthplace nor 'ethnic origin' are very accurate proxies for 'black'). Of the British population in 1971 1.2 million were enumerated as born in the New Commonwealth. When the estimated figures for those born in the New Commonwealth who were white (0.3 million) are excluded and the estimates for those born in Britain who are black are included (0.5 million), the total black population is 1.4 million in 1971.

The breakdown by country of origin (Fig. 1.2) shows the largest group to be from the Caribbean (popularly referred to as the West

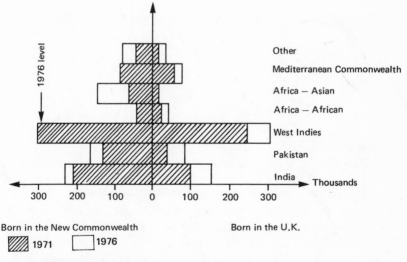

Source: OPCS Immigrant Statistics Unit, 'Country of birth and colour 1971-4', *Population Trends*, 1975, 2.

Fig. 1.2   Population of New Commonwealth and Pakistani ethnic origin by ethnic origin and birthplace, Great Britain mid 1971 and mid 1976.

Indies). Also, because immigrants from the Caribbean began to arrive for the most part before immigrants from the Indian subcontinent there are a large proportion of people of West Indian origin who were born here. By contrast, the numbers of those of Pakistani or Indian origin born in this country are small. It is estimated that 35% of the total black population in 1971 were born in the UK.

There have been various changes since 1971. The mid-year estimate of the black population in 1977 was 1.85 million, which

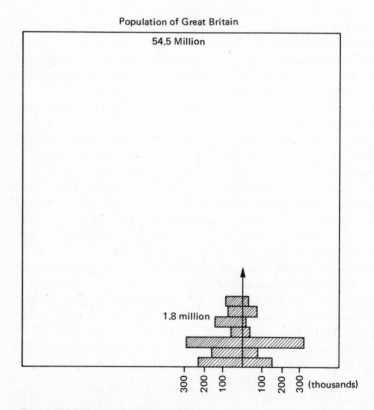

Source: OPCS Immigrant Statistics Unit, 'New Commonwealth and Pakistani Population Estimates'; Population Trends, 1977, 9.

Fig. 1.3 Population of New Commonwealth and Pakistani ethnic origin in relation to the total population of Great Britain, mid 1976.

constitutes 3.4% of the total population. At the end of the period 1971–7 West Indians formed a smaller proportion of the total than at the beginning, although they are still the largest single group. East African Asians increased most in numbers over the period as a result of the expulsion of Asians from Uganda in 1972. It is estimated that approximately 40% of the total black population in 1976 were born here. The size of the black population needs to be placed in perspective by comparing it with the total population of Britain, about 55 million. Fig. 1.3 shows this by means of a scaled down version of Fig. 1.2 so that the size of the black population is in correct proportion to the total. This shows how small the black population is compared with the total population overall. Table 1.1 gives the year-by-year black population since mid 1966.

The black population is numerically larger in some areas of the country than others. For example, there are many blacks in Bradford but few in Barnsley.[2] The areas in which black people live is a consequence of where immigrants settled in the 1950s and 1960s. These immigrants went to the large conurbations, particularly London and areas in the South East where there was a demand for labour. They also went to the metal manufacturing industries in the West Midlands and the textile industries in the North West. Fig. 1.4 shows where black people were living in 1971. The largest numbers are in the South East, followed by the Midlands. These numbers need to be seen in relation to the population as a whole, the South East being a more densely populated region. If the black population is expressed as a percentage of the total population for each region, the percentage for the West Midlands is not very different from that for the South East. A more detailed breakdown by district (Table 1.2 and Fig. 1.5) reveals considerable variations within these regions. (Birthplace data is used here as it is the only available data.) In the London boroughs the New Commonwealth born population varied between 1% of the total population in Havering and 14% in Haringey. Brent, Haringey, Lambeth, Ealing, Hackney and Islington all have more than 10% of the population born in the New Commonwealth. Within these London boroughs, too, the majority of the New Commonwealth born were to be found in a few wards, the most highly concentrated being the Northcote wards of Ealing, where approximately 50% of the population were New Commonwealth born. Outside the South East region, there are concentrations in the West Midlands region (particularly Wolverhampton, Birmingham and Coventry), West Yorkshire (particularly Bradford) and the East Midlands

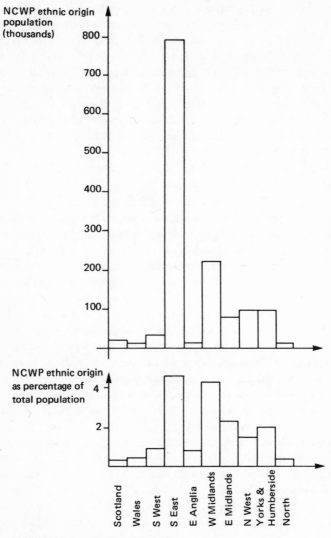

Great Britain in 1971

NCWP ethnic origin population (thousands)

NCWP ethnic origin as percentage of total population

Scotland Wales S West S East E Anglia W Midlands E Midlands N West Yorks & Humberside North

Source: Same as for figs. 1.2 and 1.3.

Fig. 1.4 Population of New Commonwealth and Pakistani ethnic origin by area of settlement, Great Britain, 1971.

Table 1.1 Estimated population of New Commonwealth and Pakistani ethnic origin in Great Britain

Mid year	NCWP (thousands)	Percentage of GB population
1966	886	1.7
1967	973	1.8
1968	1087	2.0
1969	1190	2.2
1970	1281	2.4
1971 (census year)	1371	2.5
1972	1453	2.7
1973	1547	2.8
1974	1615	3.0
1975	1691	3.1
1976	1771	3.3
1977	1846	3.4
1978	1920	3.5

(*Source:* Same as for Fig 1.3)

Table 1.2 Population born in New Commonwealth 1971 (areas with more than 20,000 NC born)

	Number of NC born (thousands)	Percentage of total population NC born
Greater London	476	6.4
Birmingham	64	6.3
Leicester	23	8.2
Bradford	23	4.9
Wolverhampton	20	7.4
Areas in Greater London with more than 20,000 NC born		
Brent	39	13.9
Haringey	35	14.4
Lambeth	33	10.9
Ealing	33	11.1
Wandsworth	26	8.9
Hackney	25	11.6
Islington	23	11.2
Newham	20	8.5

(*Source:* 1971 Census.)

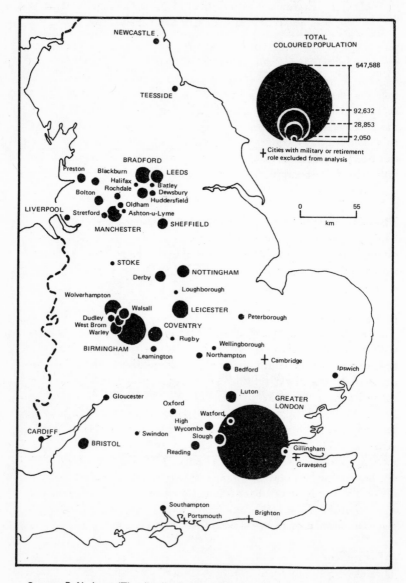

Source: P. N. Jones 'The distribution and diffusion of the coloured population in England and Wales 1961–71' Transactions Institute of British Geographers, New Series, Vol. 3, No. 4, 1978.

Fig. 1.5   Distribution of the total coloured population, 1971.

(Leicester). In each of these areas there are particular wards where about one-third of the population are New Commonwealth born.

By referring to the distribution of the black population we are passing over the different geographical distribution of the West Indian, Indian and Pakistani populations. West Indians have not necessarily settled in the same areas as Pakistanis or Indians. To take two West Yorkshire cities as an example, in Bradford there are more Pakistanis than any other group whereas in Leeds there are more West Indians. There are historical and economic reasons for this. The degree of concentration is discussed in Chapter 4. In sum, the black population is small relative to the total population size although in certain regions, cities and wards there are visible concentrations.

The demographic characteristics of the black population

This section looks at Britain's black population in greater detail giving information about such characteristics as age, sex and marital status and comparing these with characteristics for Great Britain as a whole.

(i) Age structure

The striking feature about the black population is that, in comparison with the total population of Great Britain, it is very young. This is a consequence of the youthfulness of past immigrants, who even now are not yet generally of retiring age. The pattern of immigration over the years has resulted in a concentration of the NCWP born population in the middle age groups: over 70% were aged 15 to 44 in 1971. In addition, 90% of the British born blacks were aged less than 15 years in 1971. Thus 41% of the black population of Great Britain were aged under 15 in 1971 and a further 49% were aged from 15 to 44. For Great Britain as a whole, these proportions were 24% and 39%. These age structures are illustrated in Fig. 1.6. In time, the age structure of the black population will become more like that of the total population of Great Britain.

(ii) Sex ratios

There are roughly equal numbers of males and females in Great Britain. For the black population, however, there are more males than females, and again this is the result of past immigration patterns. The shortage of women is particularly noticeable amongst Asians, especially those from Pakistan and Bangladesh for whom sex

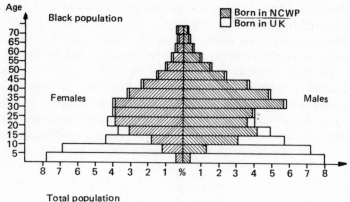

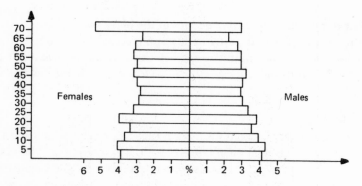

Source: Census, 1971.

Fig. 1.6   Age structure of black and total populations, Great Britain, 1971.

ratios were greater than two males for every female in 1971. This imbalance in the sex ratios should have been reduced to some extent since 1971 as a result of the concentration of women among recent immigrants. As the Asian populations become more settled in this country, the sex ratios will become more balanced; this has already happened amongst the West Indian population and to some extent amongst the Indian population.

(iii) Marital status

In 1971, 67% of the adult population who were born in the NCWP were married. 29% were single and the remaining 4% were widowed or divorced. This compares with total population figures for England and Wales of 67% married, 22% single and 11% widowed or divorced. These differences in percentages of single and widowed or divorced reflect the differing age structures of the two populations: a younger population is expected to have comparatively more single and fewer widowed or divorced people than is an older population.

The marital status by sex distributions of each minority population provide a clearer picture (Fig. 1.7). For the single NCWP born population (aged 15 and over) as a whole, there were 1.5 males to every female in 1971. For those born in India, this ratio reaches almost 2 to 1, whilst for those born in Pakistan and Bangladesh it is

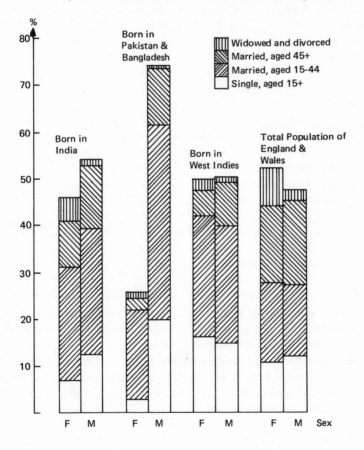

Source: Census, 1971.

Fig. 1.7 Marital status and sex of the NCWP born population aged 15 and over, England and Wales, 1971 (percentages).

higher than 6 to 1. The single Asian born population is thus comprised largely of males, many of whom cannot find wives in this country because of the much smaller numbers of single Asian women. This is an entirely different picture to the West Indian born population where there are roughly equal proportions of single females and males. This balance between the sexes is a result of the earlier migration of both women and men from the West Indies, though it differs from the single population of England and Wales in its slight preponderance of females. (In England and Wales, there are fewer single females (aged 15+) largely because women tend to marry earlier than men. This factor is probably also true of the minority populations and accounts for some of the imbalance in the sex ratios of the single Asian born).

The marked shortage of single Asian born women in Britain means that many men have to seek wives in their country of origin, and it is these women who enter the UK as fiancées or as wives (see Home Office Statistics section). Statistics on immigration show that some men also enter the country as fiancés, suggesting that for the present generation marriages are being arranged in the traditional way through the social network in the area from which they and/or their parents came. Recent changes in the Immigration Rules will severely restrict this practice, however (see Chapter 2).

Among the married NCWP born population in 1971, males again outweighed females (except those aged from 15 to 44 and born in the West Indies). Fig. 1.7 shows that this imbalance is again greatest for those born in Pakistan and Bangladesh for whom sex ratios are 2 to 1 for those aged from 15 to 44, and 5 to 1 for those aged 45+. These ratios indicate the extent to which many Asian men had yet to bring their wives to the UK in 1971. The entry of wives into Britain from the Indian sub-continent since 1971 will have partially helped to redress this situation.

The incidence of marriages between blacks and whites is more common between black men and white women than the converse. It has been estimated that among married Asians, 5% of men and 2% of women were married to a white person in 1974. Among West Indians, these figures were 8% of men and 1% of women.[3]

(iv) Births and birthrates

The annual total number of births occurring in Great Britain fell by 240,000 from 1970 to a level of 630,000 in 1977 (Fig. 1.8). The number of births to women born in India, Pakistan and Bangladesh

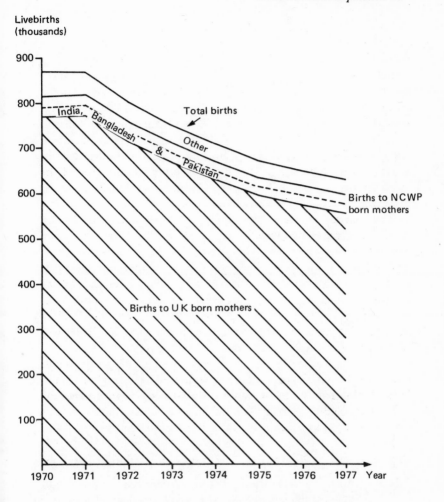

Source: OPCS Monitor FM1 Series, Births by Birthplace of Parents, HMSO
Registrar General, Scotland (1970-1977) Annual Report, Part 2. HMSO.

Fig. 1.8   Live births by birthplace of mother, Great Britain, 1970–7.

remained at 20–22,000 per year from 1970 to 1976 and increased to
23,000 in 1977. In contrast, births to West Indian born women have
fallen drastically from 14,100 in 1970 to only 6900 in 1977. These
figures include about 12.5% white births since some of the women
born in the NCWP are white, and therefore the number of births to
women of NCWP birth *and* origin is smaller than this. Apart from

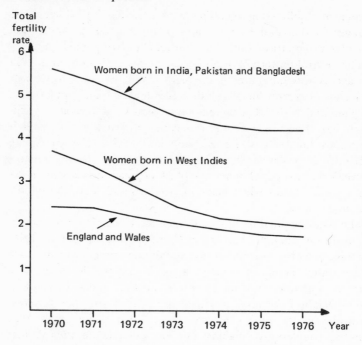

Source: L. Iliffe, 'Estimated fertility rates of Asian and West Indian immigrant women in Britain', *Journal of Biosocial Science*, 1978, 10, 189-97.
Note: Iliffe's figures are here updated to 1976. Data on numbers of women by age by birthplace are not available for 1976.

Fig. 1.9   Estimated total fertility rates, 1970–6.

this factor, the numbers of births to women born in India, Pakistan and Bangladesh reflect quite accurately the total number of births to Asian women in Great Britain, because Asians born in this country are not yet generally old enough to bear children themselves. For the West Indian population, this is less true because some of the mothers of current births were born here themselves. This group is small, however: in 1971 only 2.9% of all black people (men as well as women) had been born in the UK and were of childbearing age. It is estimated that in the mid 1970s only about 2–3000 births a year occurred to black people who were born in this country, most of them of West Indian origin.[4]

Consideration of numbers of births alone, however, gives only part of the picture and can be misleading. To gain a clearer impression, births should be considered in relation to the number of women of childbearing age. This is done in Fig. 1.9 which shows changes in the total fertility rates of the black populations and provides a comparison both over time and between populations.[5]

The general pattern of declining birthrates in Britain (until 1977 at least) is also found among the black population: indeed, the rate of decline is greater for blacks than it is for the total population of England and Wales. The population of West Indian origin, in particular, has shown a remarkable decline, so that the 1976 level is almost as low as that for England and Wales. The remaining difference is probably entirely a result of social class differences between the two populations: the black population is largely in the lower social classes which have higher birthrates than the middle and upper classes.

The Asian population has also experienced a drastic reduction in its birthrate, though there is evidence of levelling off in 1976. Examination of numbers of births and of immigration statistics (see Home Office Statistics section) suggests that this levelling off is partly a consequence of the recent arrival from India, Bangladesh and especially Pakistan of increased numbers of wives and fiancées. Birthrates in the mid 1970s may be inflated to the extent that reunited couples are 'making up' for lost time in their family building, and that newly married couples are immediately starting their families. More recent figures are not available, but it is expected that as the Asian populations, especially that of Pakistani origin, become more settled, their birthrates will begin to decline again.

(v) Deathrates
Relatively speaking, very few deaths occur among the black population. The deathrate (deaths per 1000 people) for people born in the NCWP (including some white people) was about 6 per 1000 in 1978 compared with about 12 per 1000 for Great Britain as a whole. Such a low rate is a direct consequence of the young age structure of the NCWP born population, most of whom are 'too young to die', and in no way reflects the health of the population. The deathrate for NCWP born people is, in fact, increasing over time as a result of the ageing of the population. Because of this difference in the age structure, the deathrate for the NCWP born population cannot be directly compared with that for the total population.

The overall deathrate for the NCWP born population conceals considerable differences according to birthplace. For the population born in India, Pakistan and Bangladesh, the deathrate in 1976 was about 9 per 1000, considerably higher than the rate of 4 per 1000 for those born in the West Indies. This difference cannot be attributed to differences in the age structures of the two populations.

The above discussion of deathrates takes no account of the black population born in Britain. A good indicator of the general health of a population is its deathrate among infants. A survey conducted in 1970 found perinatal mortality rates (losses in the period from 28 weeks after conception to one week after birth per 1000 births) of 31.7 and 23.1 for single births to mothers born in India, Pakistan and Bangladesh and in the West Indies respectively. This is compared with a rate of 21.3 for UK born mothers.[6]

Immigration

There are two official sources of information on immigration. These are the Control of Immigration Statistics, published by the Home Office, referred to here as Home Office Statistics, and the International Passenger Survey (IPS), conducted by the Office of Population Censuses and Surveys on behalf of the Department of Trade and Industry.

These two sets of statistics are collected for different purposes, by different means, and use different definitions. Not surprisingly, therefore, published statistics from the two sources cannot be reconciled. This is the joint Home Office and OPCS official view.[7] These problems are further discussed in Chapter 7, while here the two sets of figures are presented separately.

Home Office Statistics

The Control of Immigration Statistics are used to monitor immigration as allowed under the 1971 Immigration Act and Rules. The categories employed thus correspond directly with legal definitions and divisions, as described in Chapter 2. About half of the total inward passenger flow is not subject to immigration control (this group includes both the Irish and 'patrials'). This is reflected in the collection of statistics: with one small exception, there are no statistics on patrials. The statistics presented here are for non-patrials, that is mostly black people.

The majority of people entering the UK do so on a temporary basis. In 1979, over 12 million foreign nationals and Commonwealth citizens *entered* the UK. In the same year, only 70,000 were *accepted for settlement*, 37,000 of whom were from the NCWP. This represents

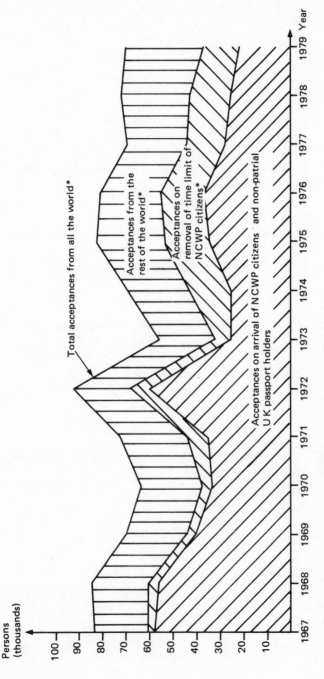

Persons
(thousands)

Total acceptances from all the world*

Acceptances from the rest of the world*

Acceptances on removal of time limit of NCWP citizens*

Acceptances on arrival of NCWP citizens and non-patrial UK passport holders

Source: Home Office, Control of Immigration Statistics, 1967-1979. HMSO Annual.

* Figures for the rest of the world underestimate the true number of people coming to the UK because many Old Commonwealth citizens and the Irish are free of immigration control.

Fig. 1.10 Acceptances for settlement in the United Kingdom, 1967–79.

a fall since 1967 of about 24,000 people per year from the NCWP. (In fact, the level of 37,000 is overestimated, and the fall correspondingly underestimated, as a result of the inflated number of recent acceptances on removal of time limit). Yet over the same period, the number from the rest of the world has risen by about 10,000 to 32,000 in 1979 (see Fig. 1.10).

Despite the overall downward trend in acceptances of NCWP citizens, there have been some temporary increases. The most notable of these, in 1972, was largely a result of the expulsion of Asians from Uganda by President Amin: these Ugandan Asians comprise 26,000 of the 35,000 UK passport holders and their dependants who were accepted for settlement on arrival in the UK from East Africa in 1972. The increases in 1975 and 1976 were caused by a variety of factors discussed in detail below.

People who are accepted for settlement fall into two broad categories: (i) acceptance for settlement on arrival in the UK, and (ii) acceptance for settlement on removal of time limit. This latter category is comprised of people who entered the UK on a temporary basis prior to their acceptance for settlement on a permanent basis. The length of time between entry and acceptance varies from less than one to many years. For this reason the annual numbers of acceptances on removal of time limit bear little relation to current immigration patterns. In addition, it should be noted that people accepted on removal of time limit appear twice in the statistics: first on entry, as temporary entrants, and secondly on acceptance for settlement.

More than 90% of the NCWP citizens (including non-patrial UK passport holders) *accepted for settlement on arrival* in 1979 were dependants, that is women, children and elderly males. The remainder were mostly holders of special vouchers which are issued only to non-patrial UK passport holders, mainly from East Africa. There was also a small number of husbands. It is likely that dependants will soon comprise almost all of those accepted on arrival. The recent decline in special voucher holders entering the UK (see Fig. 1.11a) suggests that there are now very few people eligible to come to the UK under this system. The acceptance of husbands on arrival began again (after being barred in 1969) in 1974 because of a change in the Immigration Rules, whereby husbands were allowed to join wives already settled in the UK. In 1977, this rule was changed, allowing husbands to enter temporarily and only allowing permanent settlement if, after twelve months, the

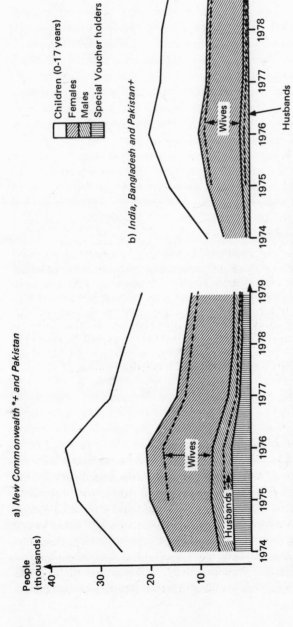

People
(thousands)

a) *New Commonwealth *+ and Pakistan*

40

30

20

10

1974 1975 1976 1977 1978 1979

Children (0-17 years)
Females
Males
Special Voucher holders

b) *India, Bangladesh and Pakistan+*

Wives

Husbands

1974 1975 1976 1977 1978 1979

Wives

Husbands

Source: Home Office, Control of Immigration Statistics, 1974–1979. HMSO Annual
* Including non-patrial UK passport holders.
+ Excluding NCW citizens with a grandparent born in the UK, most of whom are white.

Fig. 1.11 Acceptances of NCWP citizens*† for settlement on arrival, 1974–9.

Home Secretary was satisfied that the marriage was genuine. The numbers accepted under this category in 1977, 1978 and 1979 were very small. Despite this, the Rules were changed again in February 1980 to further restrict entry (see Chapter 2).

The preponderance of dependants amongst those accepted for settlement on arrival arises from past immigration patterns reinforced by legislation. Early migration from the NCWP consisted mainly of young males (but did include some young females from the West Indies) accepted for employment and settlement in the UK. Mainly because of the stricter controls imposed by the British government, this pattern has changed to the present one of mainly dependants. Because under the provisions of the *1971 Immigration Act* only those people with UK passports or with familial connections with people already in the UK are eligible for acceptance on arrival, the number of acceptances will decline in future years. In other words, the *1971 Immigration Act* ensures that immigration of this type will eventually cease.

Dependants account for all but 1 or 2% of recent acceptances on arrival of citizens of India, Bangladesh and Pakistan (see Fig. 1.11b). The speeding up of the processing of their applications in their countries of origin led to an increase in acceptances of mainly wives and children in 1975 and 1976. From 1977, however, there has been a decline in the numbers of dependants arriving from India, Bangladesh and especially Pakistan. Acceptances on arrival from the West Indies are also mainly women and children. The main feature here, however, is the small numbers involved: only 685 West Indians were accepted for settlement on arrival in 1979.

The annual number of *acceptances of NCWP citizens for settlement on removal of time limit* is considerably smaller than the number accepted on arrival (see Fig. 1.12a). From 1974 to 1977 the largest category comprised those people exempted from deportation by virtue of the fact that they had been resident in the UK for five years and were resident here on 1 January 1973. Because this includes most of those people who came to this country in the 1950s and 1960s, before immigration controls were imposed, these numbers do not represent real acceptances for settlement in the same sense as acceptances of recent immigrants. Rather, this is merely a case of the government putting its house in order by officially accepting people who were allowed to settle long ago. The effect on the statistics of this five-year residency rule is short-lived because only those resident on 1 January 1973 are eligible: after 1 January 1978 no one has been newly eligible

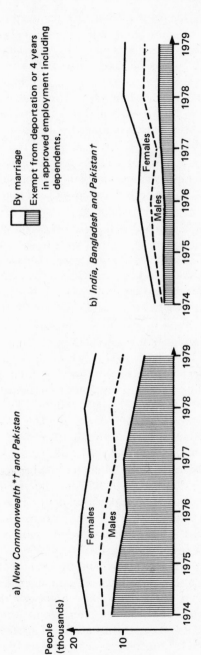

a) *New Commonwealth*† and Pakistan*

b) *India, Bangladesh and Pakistan†*

Females

Males

People (thousands)

20

10

1974 1975 1976 1977 1978 1979

☐ By marriage

▨ Exempt from deportation or 4 years in approved employment including dependents.

Source: Home Office, Control of Immigration Statistics, 1974—1979. ref. 8. HMSO Annual
* Including non-patrial UK passport holders.
† Excluding NCW citizens with a grandparent born in the UK, most of whom are white.

Fig. 1.12 Acceptances of NCWP citizens*† for settlement on removal of time limit, 1974–9.

for acceptance under this rule, so that from 1978 the numbers will decline considerably (and in any case will comprise only those people who, though eligible to claim acceptance by 1 January 1978, did not do so until later). Evidence of this can already be seen in the 1978 level: only 3400 people were accepted in that year compared to about 7000 per year in the previous four years. The dependants of these people also appear in the statistics as 'other' acceptances on removal of time limit. In 1979, the total number of those exempted from deportation and all dependants (i.e. 'others') was 3311.

The number of people accepted for settlement on completion of four years in approved employment is small but rising. This is because acceptance under this category was introduced under the *1971 Immigration Act* which came into force in January 1973. The numbers of acceptances in 1979 were 2282. As the time limit involved is four years, these figures reflect the number of work permits first issued four years ago. The number of new work permits issued annually has been falling since 1974, suggesting that the number of people accepted under this category will also decline in the future. The dependants of these people are also included in the statistics as 'other' acceptances on removal of time limit. The total number of

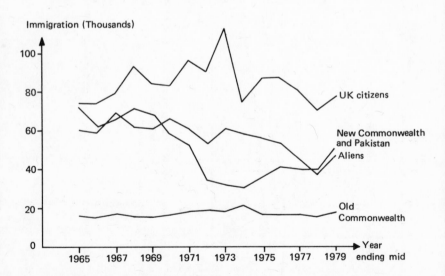

Source: OPCS, *International Migration 1974*; London HMSO, 1977. And *International Migration,* 1976; London: HMSO, 1979

Fig. 1.13   Immigration to the UK by citizenship.

'other' acceptances was about 2–3000 per year from 1975 to 1978. For 1974 and 1979, these figures are not published separately.

The annual number of acceptances by marriage of females from the NCWP has slowly risen to about 5000 in 1979. Part of this increase is a consequence of increased numbers of women from India, Bangladesh and especially Pakistan (see Figs. 1.12a and 1.12b). The time limit involved in acceptance by marriage for

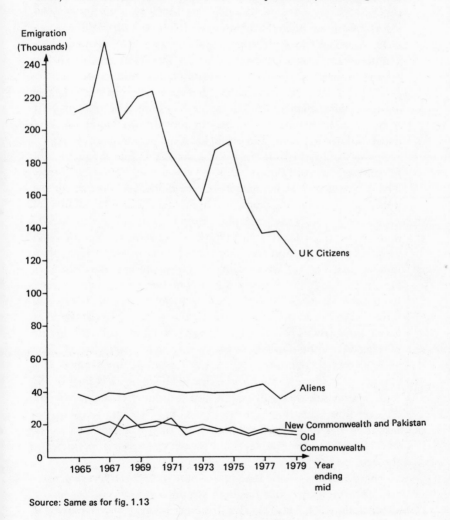

Source: Same as for fig. 1.13

Fig. 1.14   Emigration from the UK by citizenship.

women is only three months, so that the number of fiancées entering the UK and the number of women accepted for settlement by marriage in any one year are virtually the same.

The increases in males accepted for settlement by marriage in 1975 and 1976 are a result of the 1974 change in the Immigration Rules, already mentioned. The 1977 change in these rules caused a temporary decline in the level of acceptances because the time limit was extended from three to twelve months. In 1978, therefore, there is a rise in acceptances to the previous levels. In 1979, 4372 fiancées from the NCWP were accepted for settlement, 3022 of whom came from India, Bangladesh or Pakistan. The 1980 change in the Immigration Rules will reduce these numbers considerably.

There has been a steady decrease in the number of West Indians accepted for settlement on removal of time limit, from 2148 in 1974 to only 578 in 1979. The numbers exempted from deportation also decreased from 1221 in 1975 to 260 in 1978.

International Passenger Survey
The IPS is a continuing sample survey carried out mainly for the purpose of estimating statistics of tourism and the balance of payments; it covers the principal air and sea routes between the UK and overseas. The IPS distinguishes between immigrants and visitors to the UK, and there are of course many more visitors than immigrants. The IPS works with the agreed international definitions for 'immigrant' and 'emigrant'. An immigrant is a person who, having lived outside the UK for at least twelve months, declares an intention to live in the UK for at least twelve months and vice versa for an emigrant. There are limitations in the data collected by the IPS because immigrants form only a very small proportion of those arriving and therefore the sample size for immigrants is small (see Chapter 7). There is thus some doubt about the accuracy of the figures although they can be taken as indicators of general trends. The results of this survey are published in two ways, by country of last residence and by citizenship. Citizenship is determined by the nationality of the passport which a traveller is carrying and these are the figures shown here.

These statistics show that black immigration reached a peak in the 1960s and since then has been steadily cut as a result of successive Immigration Acts (Fig. 1.13). Immigration of NCWP citizens in 1967/8 was 71,000 and this number had fallen to 39,000 in 1977/8. This number does not include UK passport holders subject to immigration control. The arrival of 26,000 Ugandan Asians in 1972/3, which was allowed for political reasons, shows up mainly in the UK citizens figures as most were UK passport holders.

These figures need to be put into perspective in two ways, by looking at immigration from other parts of the world and by looking at emigration. If we look at the changes between 1967 and 1977, immigration fell overall but the most dramatic decrease was in the number of NCWP immigrants. In 1967/8, of a total of 241,000 immigrants, 71,000 were NCWP citizens (29%). In 1977/8, of a total of 162,000 immigrants, 39,000 were NCWP citizens (24%). The figures for total immigration in 1977 are the lowest recorded by the survey since it started in 1964.

Emigration from the UK is much higher than immigration (Fig. 1.14). For many years Australia and New Zealand have been the most popular countries to which emigrants have gone, but this has been reduced in recent years as a result of new and much more restrictive immigration policies introduced by these countries in late 1974 and early 1975.

On balance there are more emigrants than immigrants. In Fig. 1.15, showing net migration, positive numbers mean more people are coming into the country than leaving and negative numbers that more people are leaving than coming in. Net migration of NCWP citizens in 1977/8 was 25,000.

The Census: a retrospective view of immigration
The Home Office statistics and IPS provide a detailed picture of immigration in the last decade. A longer term view is possible from the 1971 Census by using the year of entry of those enumerated.[8] The figures used here are for those born in the New Commonwealth with one or both parents born in the New Commonwealth (this excludes most white people born in the New Commonwealth because their parents worked there). Fig. 1.16 gives the year of entry for immigrants born in the two main areas of black immigration. It shows the peak of postwar black immigration in the early 1960s and how this was reduced as a result of the *1962 and 1968 Immigration Acts*. It also shows the temporary increase in immigration immediately prior to the Acts: in other words, legislative action to control black immigration has had the effect of actually increasing immigration for short periods.[9] During this period there were more male immigrants than female. This trend was slowly reversed in the late 1960s as primary immigration was substantially reduced. There

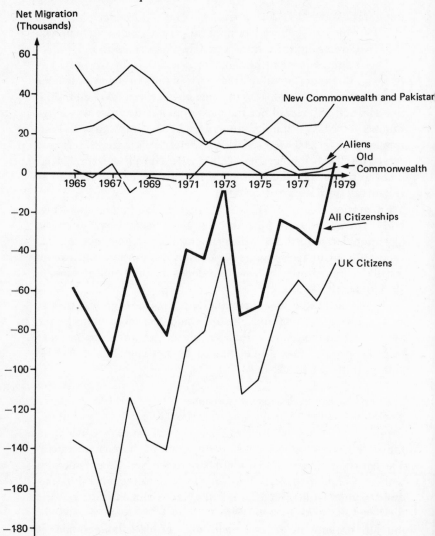

Source: Same as for fig. 1.13

Fig. 1.15 Net migration between the UK and the rest of the world by citizenship.

were particularly few Pakistani and African women arriving relative to the number of men. The early immigration from the West Indies can be seen in Fig. 1.16. This was also the first immigration to decline.

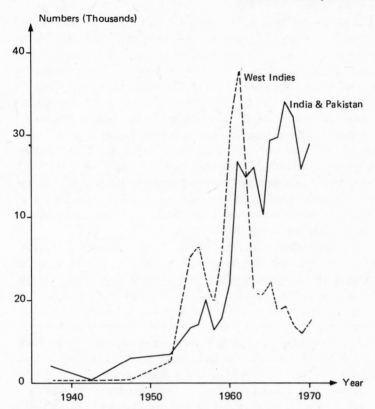

Source: G. B. Lomas, *Census 1971: The Coloured Population of Great Britain;*
London, Runnymede Trust, 1974.

Fig. 1.16 Population with one or both parents born in the West Indies or India and Pakistan by date of entry into the UK, Great Britain, 1971.

Future population size

By the year 2000, there are expected to be about 3.3 million people of NCWP origin living in Great Britain.[10] Estimates have also been produced by OPCS and these are in broad agreement with those of Brass.[11] This means that about 1 in 17, or 5.9% of the total population, will be black, an increase from the present level of about 1 in 30 or 3.3%. This increase may be attributed to the fact that the total population of Great Britain will remain roughly the same size, whilst the black population will increase by about 1.4 million. This estimate is based on recent trends in births and deaths, and on the level of immigration expected if existing legislation remained in force.

Changes in the law, in the direction of stricter controls, would obviously reduce the number of immigrants, but not by an appreciable amount because the number expected to enter is small. Even if all immigration of NCWP citizens were to cease immediately the estimate for the year 2000 would be reduced by only about 0.6 million.

After the year 2000, the proportion of black people in the total population of Great Britain is expected to remain at a stable level of about 6%. This is because net migration will be small, and because the present demographic differences which exist between the black and white populations will have effectively disappeared. The age structure of the black population will more closely resemble that of the already stable white population, and the present differential in fertility is also expected to have disappeared.

Future immigration to the UK of people from NCWP is expected to decline, since the present immigration legislation is designed to reduce such immigration over time. Eligibility to enter the UK depends on existing connections with the UK, thus ensuring that there is a limit to the number eligible. Almost all dependants and non-patrial UK passport holders will have come to the UK by the year 2000; therefore, the future NCWP immigration will be extremely small. Signs of the decline in such immigration can already be seen in the recent decrease in the number of dependants entering the UK. In the long run, a downward trend is also expected in the number of people entering as fiancées and fiancés, mainly from India, Pakistan and Bangladesh. The inevitable future balance of the sex ratios may reduce the need to find fiancées from abroad. In addition, marriage partners may more likely be found among the Asian population within Britain rather than from abroad. Restrictive changes in immigration rules and possible changes in attitudes towards arranged marriage would obviously have the same effect.

Notes
1. We here use 'New Commonwealth' (NC) to refer to those ex-British colonies, most of which now belong to the Commonwealth, whose citizens can be described as black. It therefore includes all Commonwealth countries except Australia, Canada and New Zealand (which comprise the Old Commonwealth). Pakistan left the Commonwealth in 1973, making it necessary to refer in places to New Commonwealth and Pakistan (NCWP).
2. We here use the term 'Asian' to refer to people born in, or whose parents were born in, India, Pakistan and Bangladesh. It also refers to those people born in East Africa of parents of Indian origin. To refer to these different national groups

collectively should not be taken to mean that they share identical cultural characteristics. There is in fact considerable social differentiation within the 'Asian' population. Use of the term 'Asian' can be justified if one wishes to signify a broad cultural difference between immigrants, or the children of immigrants, from the Indian sub-continent (and from East Africa) and those from the Caribbean.

3. D. J. Smith, *The Facts of Racial Disadvantage: A National Survey* (London: Political and Economic Planning, 1976).

4. OPCS Immigrant Statistics Unit, 'Marriage and birth patterns among the New Commonwealth and Pakistani population', *Population Trends*, 1978, No. 11.

5. The total fertility rate takes into account the age structure of the female population of childbearing age, and represents the average completed family size in the hypothetical situation where current fertility rates apply over the whole span of the childbearing ages. This is *not* equal to actual completed family size because fertility rates are continually changing. The rates presented here relate births by birthplace of mother to women of birthplace, so that the inclusion in the data of white births to white NCWP born mothers is effectively taken care of.

6. R. Chamberlain et al., *British Births 1970, Volume 1: The First Week of Life* (London: Heinemann Medical Books, 1975).

7. OPCS, *Immigration Statistics: Sources and Definitions*, Occasional Paper no. 15 (HMSO, 1979).

8. G. B. Lomas, *Census 1971: The Coloured Population of Great Britain* (London: Runnymede Trust, 1973).

9. C. Peach, *West Indian Migration to Britain* (London: Oxford University Press, 1968).

10. W. Brass, 'Welcome and Keep Out . . . the two signs on Britain's door', *The Listener*, 15 September 1977.

11. OPCS Immigrant Statistics Unit, 'Population of New Commonwealth and Pakistani Ethnic Origin: New Projections', *Population Trends*, 1979, No. 16.

2 Government Legislation and Policy

The strongest influence in government policy in the field of race relations has been fear of white racism and its main instrument immigration control. To a large extent the current size and social characteristics of Britain's black population, as described in Chapter 1, has been structured by the government's immigration legislation. On the other hand, accumulative evidence about racial discrimination and racial disadvantage has led the government to introduce anti-discrimination legislation and take a number of initiatives to tackle urban deprivation. This chapter summarises the three distinct aspects of government policy: immigration control, anti-discrimination legislation and attempts to combat urban deprivation.

Immigration control

In order to understand the development of legislative control over immigration,[1] it is necessary to begin with reference to the *British Nationality Act 1948*. This legislation was a response to the independence of India and clearly aimed to establish the rights of inhabitants of British colonies and Commonwealth countries to enter, work and settle in Britain. The Act established two apparently separate but actually overlapping categories of British citizenship, that of the United Kingdom and Colonies and that of the Commonwealth. The former category encompassed all those persons who had been or who were entitled to hold a United Kingdom passport, whether issued in London or from a High Commission in a dependent colony. This reflected the fact that under the *Imperial Act 1914* everyone born within the allegiance of the Crown in any part of the empire was thereby a natural-born British subject. The latter category of citizenship included the citizens of ex-colonies which had subsequently become members of the Commonwealth. Until 1947 Australia, New Zealand and Canada constituted the Commonwealth but during the

1950s and 1960s most of the British colonies achieved formal independence and also joined the ranks of Commonwealth countries so that their citizens thereby became Commonwealth citizens. These ex-colonies subsequently became known as the New Commonwealth. Commonwealth citizens were defined as having the status of British subject and so were entitled to travel to and settle in Britain without restriction. Once in Britain, such persons enjoyed equal rights with United Kingdom citizens and could acquire United Kingdom citizenship after a qualifying period of residence.

The distinction therefore had no differential effect on immigration. The 1948 Act ensured the right of colonial passport holders as well as those holding passports issued by independent Commonwealth countries to enter the United Kingdom freely, to settle and find work and to enjoy full political and social rights. The only persons subject to immigration control were 'aliens', that is citizens of countries which had no direct political ties with Britain.

It was within the legal framework established by the 1948 Act that the bulk of migration from the Caribbean and a very substantial part of that from India, Pakistan and what is now Bangladesh (collectively referred to as the Indian sub-continent) to Britain occurred. But it was not the legal possibility of entry which encouraged the migration. Poverty and unemployment in the colonies and ex-colonies, the closing of doors of entry to other countries and the demand for labour in Britain were the prime reasons for migration while the 1948 Act made it legally possible. The crucial role of labour demand is exemplified by the fact that one can trace an almost exact correlation between the level of migration from the New Commonwealth and the number of unfilled vacancies in the late 1950s.[2] During the early 1950s, a small number of MPs did raise the question of introducing controls over the entry of New Commonwealth citizens but this was not taken seriously by the leadership of either the Labour or the Conservative party. Indeed, in 1955 the Conservative government rejected the idea of immigration control as a matter of principle.

The political pressure for control seems to have increased during the late 1950s. The relatively large increase in migration from India and Pakistan in 1956/7 encouraged the Government to seek a voluntary agreement with these two countries whereby they took some responsibility for regulating migration. Then in 1958, black people were physically attacked in Nottingham and London and this was followed a year later by the intervention of Sir Oswald Mosley (formerly the leading member of the British Union of Fascists) and the Union Movement in the 1959 General Election. In the Midlands of England, both local pressure groups and MPs were vociferous proponents of controlling New Commonwealth immigration. However, the continuing debate about control worried prospective migrants, so many decided that they should migrate to Britain before controls were introduced. In sum, the talk of introducing legislation brought about just the situation that it was supposed to prevent. In 1961, the Conservative government decided on a change of policy and later in that same year introduced a bill to control the entry of Commonwealth citizens into Britain.

The beginnings of the present system of immigration controls, however, can be found as early as 1905 when the *Aliens Act 1905* was introduced to control the inflow of destitute Jewish immigrants fleeing from Central Europe and Russia. This Act was replaced by the *Aliens Restriction Act 1914* which brought more thorough control over the admission, movements and activities of aliens during the war period. In 1919, powers under the 1914 Act were renewed for a year and they were renewed annually thereafter in the form of Orders until the introduction of the *Immigration Act 1971*.

The Aliens Act and the Orders which derived from it did not apply to Commonwealth citizens who, because of their status of British subject, were allowed to enter Britain unconditionally. *The Commonwealth Immigrants Act 1962*, however, qualified the right of free entry for Commonwealth citizens. Henceforth, Commonwealth citizens and United Kingdom citizens whose passports were not issued in the United Kingdom had to obtain a Ministry of Labour employment voucher. The Ministry of Labour employment voucher scheme initially provided for three categories of voucher. Category A vouchers were issued to Commonwealth citizens who had a specific job to come to in Britain. Category B vouchers were issued to Commonwealth citizens who possessed a recognised skill or qualification which was in short supply in Britain. Category C vouchers were available to all other applicants (i.e. semi- and unskilled) with priority treatment being given to those who had served in the British armed forces during the Second World War, and thereafter on a 'first come first served' basis.

During the debate on the Bill in the House of Commons, the Labour Party opposed it on a point of principle and claimed that it was inspired by racist sentiment, pointing to the fact that the Bill made no attempt to place controls on immigration from the Republic of Ireland (which was not even a member of the Commonwealth and yet whose citizens had a free right to enter and work in Britain). However, opposition in principle was to soon become pragmatic acceptance of immigration control of persons from the New Commonwealth.

The 1962 Act did not impose control over the migration to Britain of citizens of the United Kingdom and Colonies who held UK passports issued by, or on behalf of, the United Kingdom government either in Britain or through a High Commission abroad. Such passports had been issued to persons of Indian origin in East Africa in the course of negotiations over the terms for independence of Kenya, Uganda and Tanzania. Even before independence, large numbers of these persons had acquired citizenship of the United Kingdom and Colonies, and although on independence, many had applied for and obtained citizenship of the new states, many others opted and obtained United Kingdom passports. In 1967, and not without warning, the Kenyan government passed legislation which stipulated that all aliens who had not opted for Kenyan citizenship could live and work in Kenya only on a temporary basis. Not surprisingly, because they were exercising the right given to them by virtue of holding a UK passport, many of these persons began to come to Britain. Certain prominent Conservative politicians began predicting the sudden arrival of a quarter of a million Asian immigrants from East Africa, whereas in reality the number was, by early 1968, 66,000.[3] The Conservative party demanded, amongst other things, that the entry of Kenyan Asians holding UK passports be phased. The Labour government went further: it removed the right of entry.

This was done by means of the *Commonwealth Immigrants Act 1968*. This Act withdrew from United Kingdom passport holders (UKPH) who lacked a 'close connection' with the United Kingdom the right of entry and settlement. 'Close connection' was defined as birth in the United Kingdom or of descent from a parent or grandparent born in the United Kingdom, or of naturalisation, registration in the United Kingdom as a citizen of the United Kingdom and Colonies, or adoption in the United Kingdom. Those UKPHs who could not demonstrate 'close connection' were placed in the same legal category as Commonwealth citizens who were already subject to strict control over entry. In addition, a voucher scheme was introduced. Possession of a voucher entitled a UKPH and his close dependants to enter and settle in Britain. The number of vouchers issued was limited to

1500 per annum, although this was increased to 3000 in 1971 in response to the political situation in Uganda.

The Act was introduced and rushed through Parliament in three days. The 'close connection' device was explicitly designed to ensure that white settlers in East Africa retained their right of entry to Britain by virtue of possession of a UK passport while black settlers, despite holding the same passport, did not. The Act was subsequently the subject of complaints to the European Commission on Human Rights.

The European Convention of Human Rights was signed in Rome on 4 November 1950, and entered into force on 3 September 1953; the United Kingdom is a signatory to the Convention and accepts the provisions that provide for states to recognise the right of individuals to petition the Commission and to accept the compulsory jurisdiction of the European Court of Human Rights. Petitions can only be sent to the Commission which first decides on the admission of an application; if the application is admitted the Commission attempts to conciliate; if this fails a report must be sent to the Committee of Ministers and may be referred to the Court for decision.

A decision of the Commission dated 10 October 1970 related to the applications of 25 East African Asians who complained that they were refused admission to the United Kingdom or permission to remain there permanently. In each of these cases the Commission declared the complaints admissible along with a further six cases in December 1970. In its reasons for admitting the complaints the Commission was most explicit in relation to Article 3 which relates to 'degrading treatment'; it stated that 'publicly to single out a group of persons for differential treatment on the basis of race might, in certain circumstances, constitute a special form of affront to human dignity'. In the light of this interpretation of the Convention and in view of its finding that the United Kingdom government 'have admitted that the intentions and the effects of the *Commonwealth Immigrant Act 1968* were discriminatory', the Commission declared the complaints admissible, but failed to reach a friendly settlement through conciliation. A confidential report was sent to the Committee of Ministers of the Council of Europe. The Committee of Ministers did not send the report for decisions by the Court of Human Rights, and did not itself take action. In October 1977 it decided to remove the examination of the case from its agenda.

The main aim of the *Immigration Appeals Act 1969* was to establish an appeal system for persons who were refused entry to Britain but while it was proceeding through Parliament, an amendment was introduced by the Labour government which made it obligatory for wives and children seeking settlement in Britain as dependants of Commonwealth citizens already resident to be in possession of an entry certificate. These certificates had been in existence since 1962, but possession of a certificate had not been a condition of entry. They were justified on the grounds that it made it possible for the persons concerned to establish that they had a right of entry and would therefore be admitted on arrival. To obtain a certificate, the prospective immigrant had to apply for an interview at the nearest British High Commission (which may be several hundred miles away). At this interview, which can be several months and even years ahead, the applicant had to prove the claimed relationship to the person legally resident in Britain, usually by possession of birth and marriage certificates. The consequence is that persons who have the legal right of entry and settlement are forced to wait months and years or are even denied entry because they are unable to produce documents which they were never issued.[4]

The most recent legislation governing immigration to Britain is the *Immigration Act 1971*, which came into force on 1 January 1973. It replaces the *Commonwealth Immigrant Acts of 1962 and 1968* and provides the framework of the current law on the control of admission to Britain. The practice to be followed in the administration of the Act is set out in the Immigration Rules which are laid before Parliament by the Home Secretary. These rules are not part of the Act itself but are drafted by the Home Secretary and are not necessarily debated by Parliament. On 20 February 1980 the *Statement of Changes in Immigration Rules* (HC 394) was laid before Parliament. This statement replaces the statements of Immigration Rules laid before Parliament on 25 January 1973 and provided for the new Rules to come into effect on 1 March 1980.

The *Immigration Act 1971* gives the 'right of abode' in Britain to people it defines as 'patrial'. They are

1. Citizens of the United Kingdom and Colonies who have that citizenship by birth, adoption, naturalisation or registration in the United Kingdom, OR who were born of parents one of whom had United Kingdom citizenship by birth etc. in the United Kingdom OR one of whose grandparents had such citizenship at the time of the birth of the relevant parent.
2. Citizens of the United Kingdom and Colonies who have at any

time been settled in the United Kingdom and who have been ordinarily resident in the United Kingdom for five years or more.

3. Commonwealth citizens (i.e. not necessarily citizens of the United Kingdom and Colonies) born or adopted by a citizen of the United Kingdom and Colonies by birth in the United Kingdom.

4. The spouse of a patrial (provided that she/he is a Commonwealth citizen).

5. The former wife of a patrial and citizens of the United Kingdom and Colonies provided that she is a Commonwealth citizen.

All aliens, and all Commonwealth citizens (including citizens of the United Kingdom and Colonies) who are not patrial, need permission to enter Britain. Those Commonwealth citizens admitted for settlement under previous legislation (i.e. persons legally resident in the United Kingdom free of controls before 1 January 1973) retain the right to bring in certain close dependants. EEC nationals may enter freely to work or to seek work; Commonwealth citizens with a United Kingdom grandparent are in practice allowed to enter freely.

Non-patrials can be admitted to Britain under differing circumstances and conditions which can be broadly divided into four categories. The main conditions of entry and settlement are outlined below:

1. Those coming for temporary purposes. These are mainly visitors and students. A visitor must satisfy the immigration officer that he/she can support him/herself and any dependants without working during the period of the visit and can meet the cost of the return or outward journey. Immigration Officers are instructed to impose a time-limit on the period of the visitor's stay (which is usually six months, but may be longer if the officer is satisfied that the visitor can maintain him/herself). A student must satisfy the immigration officer that he/she has been accepted for a course of study at a bona fide educational institution, that the course will occupy the whole or a substantial part of his/her time, and that he/she can meet the cost of the course and his/her own maintenance. A time limit of twelve months is normally imposed but may be extended on application to the Home Secretary, if the conditions attached to leave to enter and remain are met.

2. Those coming for employment or business purposes. Persons coming for employment must have a work permit issued by the

Department of Employment in respect of a specific post with a specific employer. Generally, permits are only issued to those with recognised skills or professional qualifications and employers have to show that they have been unable to recruit suitable workers from among the resident workforce. In addition, there is a quota system for the issue of permits to workers in hotels and catering, resident domestic workers and nursing auxiliaries in hospitals, workers from Malta and other dependent territories and UK passport holders. In 1978 the total number of work permits available for all these categories was 4100. The government intends to abolish completely the quota for hotel and catering.

The work permit system does not apply to certain categories of employment, e.g. ministers of religion, doctors and dentists, representatives of overseas newspapers, persons coming for employment in a government department. There is also an exception for Commonwealth citizens who can prove that at least one of their grandparents was born in the United Kingdom. Such a person wishing to take up employment in Britain will be granted an entry clearance for that purpose (and so does not need a work permit) and will normally be given indefinite leave to enter.

Broadly speaking, if a businessman wishes to join an established business or to set up a business on his/her account, he/she has to show that he/she has adequate finance and will not need employment for which a work permit is required.

3. Those coming for settlement. In this category there are four main groups of people who are permitted to settle permanently upon arrival. First, there are the New Commonwealth and Pakistan wives and children under 18 years whose husband/father settled in Britain before 1 January 1973. Those who settle after this date are entitled under the Rules to have their wives and children join them, but they must prove that they can support and house them without recourse to public funds. All such persons must possess an entry certificate. Second, the husband/fiancé of a woman settled in Britain will only be accepted for permanent settlement if the wife or fiancée is a citizen of the UK and Colonies who was born in the UK or one of whose parents was born in the UK. Third, there are parents, grandparents and distressed relatives. Parents and grandparents can only be admitted if the father/grandfather is over 65 (no age restriction in the case of a widow) and they are wholly or mainly dependent on their child/grandchild and he/she is willing and able to support

them. Such persons must have an entry certificate. Distressed relatives must also fulfil these conditions. In addition, they must show that they have no relatives in their country of residence and are virtually destitute. Fourth, there are non-patrial UKPHs (i.e. the category created by the *1968 Commonwealth Immigration Act*) who can only enter and settle upon production of a special voucher as previously explained. The number of vouchers issued annually was increased from 3000 to 5000 in 1975. In 1976 it was estimated that there were no more than 38,000 such persons in East Africa, although it is not known how many of these would wish to come to Britain.

In addition to persons accepted for settlement on arrival certain categories of people are given limited leave to enter and may subsequently be accepted for settlement on removal of time limit. This category largely consists of those accepted for settlement by reason of marriage.

4.   The Irish and EEC nationals. There is no control over immigration from Ireland. Indeed the Irish are the largest immigrant group in the United Kingdom. By virtue of the United Kingdom membership of the European Economic Community and the *European Communities Act 1972*, the provisions of the Treaty of Rome relating to the free movement of labour have effect in the United Kingdom. EEC nationals may enter Britain free of immigration control for six months to seek work. If, after six months, they have found work, they may apply for residence permits.

An important effect of the *Immigration Act 1971* is to put workers from New Commonwealth countries on the same footing as workers from other overseas countries (other than those from the Irish Republic or other EEC countries). They have become subject to control by annual work permit, and thus to the possibility of non-renewal of the permit. Whereas Commonwealth workers previously admitted under employment vouchers had the right to settle, under this Act they have no right to stay on. After four years of working in approved employment they can, however, apply for conditions to be removed.

The Act itself is administered through immigration rules and the effect of the rules has been to limit the numbers of certain groups of immigrants – mainly coloured New Commonwealth citizens – seeking to enter this country for work and settlement. Under the Act, all aliens and all Commonwealth citizens who are not 'patrial' need permission to enter Britain. As the majority of nationals of New

Commonwealth countries are unlikely to have parents or grand-parents born in Britain, it is this group of immigrants who have been most affected by the new regulations; immigrants from the Old Commonwealth countries, Australia, Canada and New Zealand, are less affected, as they are more likely to have the right of patrial status by descent.

The anti-discrimination legislation

The anti-discrimination legislation represented a radical departure from the tradition of the British legal system. Britain stands alone among Western societies in having no Bill of Rights or written con-stitution to guarantee equal protection of the law. *The Race Relations Acts of 1965, 1968 and 1976* were a significant step in that direction. It was an attempt to influence behaviour and attitudes by a law which declared that everyone in Britain was henceforth to be treated on the basis of individual merit, regardless of colour or race.

The first attempt to legislate against racial discrimination in public places in Britain was made in a private member's Bill intro-duced in 1951 by a Labour MP, Mr Reginald (later Lord) Sorenson. In the years between 1952 and 1964 Lord Brockway made ten attempts to persuade Parliament to legislate on the subject. From 1960 onwards, the support for legislation widened to include members of both parties, and after the use of physical violence against black people in London and Nottingham in 1958, the Labour Party issued a statement urging the Conservative govern-ment to outlaw 'the public practice of discrimination' and pledged the next Labour government to introduce such legislation.

The Race Relations Act 1965, set up conciliation machinery to deal with complaints of discrimination and made unlawful, discrimination on the grounds of 'race, colour, ethnic or national origin' in such places as hotels, restaurants, places of entertainment or on public transport. The conciliation machinery was invested in the Race Relations Board which had a chairman and two other members appointed by the Home Secretary, and seven conciliation committees (on all of which there was trade unions representation) to consider complaints about alleged discrimination. The number of complaints made to the Race Relations Board were small, and a large proportion fell outside the scope of the Act. It became clear from a number of enquiries, most notably the study 'Anti-Discrimination legislation', by Professor Harry Street, Geoffrey Howe, QC, and Geoffrey Bindman, published by PEP (1967), which studied the American and Canadian experience and made certain proposals including (i) that legislation must deal with the worst problems, namely housing and employment; and (ii) that the legislation must contain adequate provision for enforcement. This led to the introduction, by the Labour government, of the *Race Relations Act 1968,* which extended the provisions of the 1965 Act to cover a wider field, notably employment, housing and the provision of services.

The *Race Relations Act 1968* aimed to deal with discrimination on grounds of 'colour, race or ethnic or national origin' in employment, housing, the provision of goods, facilities of services to the public and the publication or display of discriminatory advertisements or notices. The Act reconstituted the Race Relations Board and gave it a duty to investigate complaints of racial discrimination. The Board also had the responsibility of resolving the dispute by conciliation; and in the event of litigation had sole power to bring proceedings. The 1968 Act also established the Community Relations Commission, which replaced the former, non-statutory body, the National Committee for Commonwealth Immigrants. Its duties were to promote harmonious community relations and to advise the Home Secretary on matters concerning community relations. The Community Relations Commission also co-ordinated the work of a number of independent local community relations councils.

The achievements of the 1968 Act were expressed by a subsequent Labour government to have been as follows:

> Generally, the law has had an important declaratory effect and has given support to those who do not wish to discriminate but who would otherwise feel compelled to do so by social pressure. It has also made crude, overt forms of racial discrimination much less common. Discriminatory advertisements and notices have virtually disappeared both from the press and from public advertisements boards. Discriminatory conditions have largely disappeared from the rules governing insurance and other financial matters and they are being removed from tenancy agreements. It is less common for an employer to refuse to accept any coloured workers and there has been some movement of coloured workers into more desirable jobs.[5]

However, evidence from reliable studies and surveys suggested that with some exceptions the legislation had been ineffective in reducing the extent of discrimination against ethnic minorities. The reports Racial Disadvantage in Employment (June 1974), and The Extent of Racial Discrimination (September 1974), published by

Political and Economic Planning (PEP), indicated that discrimination in employment, in particular, was widespread. Comparison of the results of the 1974 study on employment with the results of a study conducted by PEP in 1967 showed that in 1974 there appeared to be a lower level of discrimination against people with high qualifications in comparison with the level in 1967; furthermore the 1974 findings showed a marked decline in discrimination against coloured potential house buyers. Despite these findings, however, and despite the fact that the *Race Relations Act 1968* had been in operation for six years by 1974, the PEP study of September 1974 found a substantial level of discrimination in all manual job recruitment: 'the tests indicated that an Asian or West Indian would, when applying for an unskilled job, face discrimination in at least a third, and perhaps as many as half of all cases' (page 14). This implied, according to the report, tens of thousands of cases annually, compared with the 150 employment complaints received by the Race Relations Board in 1973.

In 1975 the Labour government identified the following weaknesses of the 1968 Act:

1. There was a marked lack of public confidence in the effectiveness of the law evidenced by no amelioration in the status of Britain's racial minorities.
2. The definition of discrimination was too narrow and did not cover areas where the effect of a practice was discriminatory, regardless of motive.
3. Individual complaints were not an adequate basis for law enforcement.
4. The Race Relations Board was hampered by the duty to investigate every complaint and was not free to pursue a strategic role.
5. The investigatory and enforcement powers of the Race Relations Board were too limited.
6. Individual cases were too slowly dealt with while the obligation to investigate every complaint had the effect of denying the individual access to the courts to obtain a direct remedy and compensation.
7. Damages awarded were derisory and injunctions were very difficult to obtain.[6]

The Race Relations Act 1976 was drafted in response to these weaknesses in the previous Act. The Race Relations Board and Community Relations Commission were dissolved and replaced by the Commission for Racial Equality. The new Commission was to have 'a major strategic role in enforcing the law in the public interest. Although it will be able to assist . . . individuals in appropriate cases, the Commission's main task will be wider policy; to identify and deal with discriminatory practices by industries, firms or institutions.'[7]

The Race Relations Act 1976 defines two kinds of racial discrimination – direct and indirect. Direct racial discrimination is said to occur when a person treats another person less favourably on 'racial grounds' than he/she treats, or would treat someone else. 'Racial grounds' refers to 'colour, race, nationality (including citizenship) or ethnic or national origins'. Indirect racial discrimination refers to treatment which may be described as equal in a formal sense as between 'racial groups' but discriminatory in its effect on one particular 'racial group'. A 'racial group' is identified by the same set of characteristics used to identify 'racial grounds'. Thus, where an employer requires applicants to pass a test before obtaining employment and that test has the effect of excluding black applicants and cannot be shown to be significantly related to the performance of the job, then that test constitutes unlawful discrimination, irrespective of the motives of the employer. In addition, the Act defines segregation on racial grounds as racial discrimination and makes it unlawful to victimise a person because he/she has asserted his/her rights under the Act.

The Act applies to employment, training and related fields, education, housing, the provision to the public of goods, facilities and services, and to the publication of discriminatory advertisements relating to activities in all these areas. In general, the provisions of the Act apply to the actions of government ministers and government departments, although there is an exclusion clause relating to existing rules restricting employment in the service of the Crown to persons of particular birth, nationality, descent or residence. The Act also applies to local authorities but they are given the additional duty of ensuring that their functions are carried out with regard to the need both to eliminate unlawful racial discrimination and to promote equal opportunity and good relations among people of different 'racial groups'.

The enforcement of the Act has two dimensions, that of the individual remedy and that of the strategic function of the Commission for Racial Equality. Concerning individual remedies, an individual who believes that he/she has been the victim of unlawful discrimination has the right to initiate proceedings in a designated county court or a sheriff court or an industrial tribunal, where appropriate. Complaints in the employment field are made to industrial tribunals while complaints in all other fields are dealt with by designated county courts in England and Wales and by sheriff courts in Scotland. Complaints relating to education have first to be notified to the Minister of Education before they can be brought to court. Individuals may in appropriate cases receive help from the Commission both in deciding whether to proceed with a case and in presenting a case in the most effective manner. A standard questionnaire is available from the Commission which is to be completed by the alleged discriminator. The Commission may give further assistance if it considers that the case rises a question of principle or is too complex for the individual to deal with unaided. The Commission itself may institute legal proceedings in respect of persistent discrimination. It alone may institute proceedings in respect of indirect discriminatory practices, discriminatory advertisements, and cases where an individual instructs or attempts to induce another to commit an act of unlawful discrimination. If an industrial tribunal finds in favour of the complainant, it may make an order declaring the rights of the parties, make an order requiring the respondent to pay the complainant compensation or recommend that the respondent take a particular course of action. In the case of the county or sheriff courts, an order declaring the rights of the parties may be made, an injunction or order may be declared, or damages may be awarded.

The Commission has the power to conduct formal investigations where discrimination is suspected. It may conduct such investigations on its own initiative or may be required to do so by the Home Secretary. The terms of reference of investigations may be wide ranging or confined to the activities of named persons. The Commission has powers, with certain limitations, to compel the production of information and the presence of witnesses. When the investigation is complete, the Commission publishes a report which may include recommendations for changes in policies and procedures or recommendations to the Home Secretary for changes in the law. If, in the course of such an investigation, the Commission becomes satisfied that a contravention of the Act has occurred, it may serve a non-discrimination notice on the person concerned, which requires not only compliance with the notice, but also the provision of information from time to time so that the Commission is able to monitor continuous compliance. In a case of persistent discrimination, the Commission may seek an injunction.

The 1976 Act does not permit what has been called 'reverse discrimination'. For example, it is not lawful to discriminate in favour of a black person in recuitment or promotion on the grounds that other black people have experienced discrimination in the past. However, the Act does permit certain limited forms of positive action. First, training bodies, employers, trade unions and employers' and professional organisations may provide special training facilities for members of 'racial groups' and encourage them to take advantage of opportunities to do particular work. This means that special training courses may be run for black people who are significantly underrepresented in a particular area of work. But, once having trained, there can be no discrimination in favour of black people when they apply for a job. Second, there is a general exemption from the entire scope of the Act for action aimed at affording persons of a particular 'racial group' access to facilities or services to meet their special needs with regard to education, training, welfare or any ancillary benefits. This would apply, for example, to a residential home for elderly Bangladeshis, English language classes for immigrants, or advice on birth control given by Indian women to Indian women. The language of this exclusion clause is broad and care must be taken in its interpretation so that it does not become the justification for, for example, 'separate but equal' facilities or quotas in education which would adversely affect black people. Third, there is a special exemption from the employment provisions of the Act in cases where the holder of a job provides persons of a particular 'racial group' with personal services promoting their welfare and where those services can most effectively be provided by a person of the same group. This would cover employment in the situations referred to in the second instance above.

Finally, the *Race Relations Act 1976* amends the *Public Order Act 1936* by inserting into it a new section which makes it a criminal offence to publish or distribute written matter or use in any public place or at any public meeting language which is threatening, abusive or insulting and which, taking account of all the circumstances, is likely to encourage hatred against a 'racial group'. An exception is made for fair and accurate reports of judicial proceedings and of proceedings in Parliament. Unlike the earlier amendment to the *Public Order*

Act 1936 made by the *Race Relations Act 1965,* which the 1976 Act replaces, it is no longer necessary to prove that the accused intended to encourage such sentiments. Incitement to 'racial hatred' is a criminal offence dealt with by the criminal courts and prosecutions can be brought only by, or with the consent of, the Attorney General. The enforcement of this section of the 1976 Act is not the responsibility of the Commission for Racial Equality.

Compared with the provisions of the *Race Relations Acts of 1965 and 1968,* the 1976 Act represents a more determined and comprehensive attempt to reduce and eliminate racial discrimination. How effective the legislation is in practice is another matter.[8] On this, the evidence is at present limited. During the first year of the operation of the Act, the Commission for Racial Equality had 862 applications for assistance. In this period, 123 tribunal decisions were received and of these, four were won by the complainants. Between June and September 1978, a further four cases were won, bringing the total number of successful cases to eight. For all these cases, the compensation awarded was in the region of £75–250. The Commission had 30 formal investigations in progress by April 1979, of which two had been completed and two non-discrimination notices had been issued. Finally, in relation to incitement to racial hatred, the Attorney General, in answer to a written question in the House of Commons on 12 December 1978, reported that the police had submitted eleven reports relating to their investigations of alleged offences. In one case, his consent to proceed with prosecution had been granted; in three other cases the Director of Public Prosecutions had advised that the evidence did not justify the instigation of proceedings; the remaining cases were still under consideration.

Urban deprivation
Racial discrimination, although still widespread, is not the only factor which is responsible for the economic and social disadvantage experienced by black people in Britain. This was recognised by the Labour government of 1974–9 in the White Paper 'Racial Discrimination' (1975) which preceded the *Race Relations Act 1976:*

> The possibility has to be faced that there is at work in this country, as elsewhere in the world, the familiar cycle of cumulative disadvantage by which relatively low-paid or low-status jobs for the first generation of immigrants go hand in hand with poor overcrowded living conditions and a depressed environment. If, for example, job opportunities, educational facilities, housing and

environmental conditions are all poor, the next generation will grow up less well equipped to deal with the difficulties facing them. The wheel then comes full circle, as the second generation find themselves trapped in poor jobs and poor housing. If, at each stage of this process an element of racial discrimination enters in, then an entire group of people are launched on a vicious downward spiral of deprivation. They may share each of the disadvantages with some other deprived group in society; but few other groups in society display all their accumulated disadvantages (page 3).[9]

The analysis in the White Paper identified two basic kinds of issue with which the government should properly concern itself. The first is the handicap with which the black communities are saddled as a consequence of outright racial discrimination. The second is the complex of 'remediable disadvantages' which minorities suffer from as a result of their relative newness, their jobs and housing conditions, their low status and their disproportionate exposure to wider urban problems. The White Paper was mainly concerned with racial discrimination and this part of government policy has been implemented. It was, however, explicitly recognised that, beyond the proposals in the White Paper, there will need to be 'a more comprehensive strategy for dealing with the related and at least equally important problem of disadvantage' (page 6). Since then the problem has been redefined as the problem of the 'inner cities' and in the late 1970s the politicians, local authorities and planners began to search for an 'inner city policy'. This should not, however, obscure the fact that for the preceding ten years the central government has been initiating policies to deal with economic and social decline in urban areas. This section provides a brief factual account of what has been attempted by central government to tackle urban deprivation and of the 'inner city' policy announced in 1977. These are arranged under the government departments responsible for each one.

(i) The Home Office
The Home Office has been responsible for the Urban Programme (1968), the Community Development Project (1969), the Urban Deprivation Unit (1973) and the Comprehensive Community Programmes (1974). In addition the Home Office is responsible for the administration of Section 11 of the *Local Government Act 1966*.

The urban Programme was first announced by the Prime Minister

in a major speech on immigration and race relations in May 1968.
He stated: 'many of our big towns face tremendous problems,
whether in housing, whether in health and welfare, even where there
is virtually no immigrant problem. Expenditure must be on the basis
of need and the immigration problem is only one factor, though a
very important factor, in the assessment of social need.' The intention
was to arrest and reverse the downward spiral of decline of such
areas. However, the amount of money available was small. A government circular distributed in October 1968 stated that £25 million
was available over a four-year period. In 1972 the sum was increased
by a futher £40 million for the period 1972–6, making a total of £65
million over eight years. In addition to the money made available by
central government, local authorities have to find one-quarter of the
cost of each project.

Funds were allocated by the Home Office on the basis of priority
lists of projects submitted by local authorities in response to circulars
sent out by the Home Office. The number of bids usually exceeded
the money available and so the Home Office had a wide discretion
as to which projects it funded. It is not easy to distinguish the
criteria which were applied in practice, although there is some
evidence to suggest a shift in emphasis since 1968 from local authority
capital projects towards greater support for voluntary organisations.
In order to illustrate the type of activity supported by the Urban
Programme, the following types of project were funded under the
Home Office's Circular 14: provision of day care facilities for families
and young children, alternative treatment for young offenders,
schemes to meet the special needs of black people, advice centres
and legal services.

In 1977 the Department of Environment was given the responsibility for administering the Urban Programme. In June 1977 the
White Paper 'Policy for the Inner Cities' announced a recasting and
enhancement of the Urban Programme.[10] The Programme was
extended to cover industrial, environmental and recreational
provision. The size of the Programme was also to be substantially
increased. Expenditure on the Urban Programme has grown
gradually throughout its life until it stood at £29.8 million in 1976/77
and £35.2 million in 1977/78 (at 1979 survey prices). In 1978/79 this
grew to £98 million; in 1979/80 £165.0 million was allocated to the
Programme. The bulk of the allocation in 1979/80 was earmarked
for the Partnership and Programme areas (see below).

The Urban Programme was not intended to deal specifically with the disadvantage of black people living in declining urban areas. Rather, black people were expected to benefit equally with other residents of such areas from the projects funded by the Home Office. Some funds have been allocated to projects which intend to deal specifically with disadvantage faced by black people, but the total amount allocated to such projects has been small: Runnymede Trust research workers estimated that the total assistance granted to such projects during the first two phases amounted to 5% of that allocated to all voluntary projects.[11]

The Community Development Project (CDP) was defined as 'a neighbourhood based experiment aimed at finding new ways of meeting the needs of people living in areas of high social deprivation'. The original aim was to encourage local self-help initiative in poor areas on the grounds that improvements could be made through increased motivation and involvement of the people living in these areas. Twelve local projects were established between 1969 and 1972 in places which ranged from the small and isolated settlement of Cleator Moor to the disadvantaged neighbourhoods of large cities such as Hillfields in Coventry and Saltley in Birmingham. All shared the characteristics of declining industry, high unemployment and bad housing. In some areas, black people formed a high proportion of the population. Each project combined research with social action designed to encourage local residents to defend their rights and articulate their needs.

The relationship between the local projects and the Home Office was neither consistent nor constructive. This partly a consequence of the fact that many of the project reports argued that deprivation was not caused by the shortcomings of the people living in the area but by structural factors which were outside their control. Accordingly, CDP reports were critical of government policy. Until May 1972 the Home Office had a central research unit which evaluated the individual projects. This was abandoned in favour of local initiative, but pressure from the projects led to the formation of a central information unit which published several inter-project reports. This was closed in September 1976 and most of its functions taken over by the Urban Deprivation Unit. All the projects have now been completed, but there has been no published overall assessment of the project as a whole.

In a debate in the House of Commons on 1 November 1973, the then Home Secretary Mr Robert Carr (now Lord Carr) announced the formation in the Home Office of a special unit to be called the

Urban Deprivation Unit. He said 'I see this work as the key to providing a better life for those who live in the cities and also as a way of improving community relations. Although the urban problem is not one which, in itself, centres on race, large numbers of our coloured citizens live in our older city areas. Therefore, if we can remove some of the stress and frustration from urban life, we shall at the same time be making an important contribution to better race relations.' The Unit was set up in two parts. The first was a research organisation to study the nature of urban deprivation and thereby to establish guidelines for policy. The second was to co-ordinate the various activities of government departments. Hence, the Unit became· the administrative centre for other government-initiated projects: it administered the Urban Programme (until 1977), the distribution of funds under Section 11 of the *Local Government Act 1966* and the Community Development Projects.

In the House of Commons on 18 July 1974, the then Home Secretary Mr Roy Jenkins announced 'a new strategy for tackling the problem of those living in the most acutely deprived urban areas'. This was to involve 'the preparation and subsequent implementation by selected local authorities, in collaboration with all those concerned, of comprehensive community programmes containing an analysis of the needs of the area considered as a whole and proposals for meeting them. Those programmes are to be developed through a series of trial runs, and financial arrangements will be discussed with the local authorities.' The aim of the trial programmes was to examine how best existing local authority and central government resources can be used to tackle urban deprivation in the context of the whole local authority area.

Under Section 11 of the *Local Government Act 1966,* local authorities may claim grant aid if they are required to employ extra staff in consequence of the presence within their areas of substantial numbers of 'immigrants' from the Commonwealth whose language and customs differ from those of the rest of the community. Authorities are not required to seek prior approval for expenditure but merely to follow the guidelines given in circulars to claim grant aid (75% payable) on relevant expenditure, including the full cost of staff salaries.

A local authority qualifies for Section 11 assistance by showing that more than 2% of its schoolchildren have parents who were born in the New Commonwealth and arrived in the UK in the preceding ten years. As the Department of Education and Science ceased demanding the collection of these statistics in 1973, grants paid after this date are based on out-of-date information. Moreover, the ten-year rule eliminates areas such as Liverpool where black people began to settle much earlier. The actual take-up of funds has been very uneven. A Community Relations Commission working party estimated that up to 1973, 53% of this expenditure had gone to just four local authorities (ILEA, Ealing, Birmingham, Bradford) which, according to 1972 DES statistics contained only 37% of 'immigrant' pupils.[12]

In November 1978 the Labour government published a consultative document, 'Proposals for Replacing Section 11 of the *Local Government Act 1966*' and in a foreword to the document the then Home Secretary Mr Merlyn Rees said that

> An important feature of the measures to help ethnic minorities in recent years has been the grant-aid power provided by Section 11 of the *Local Government Act 1966* which was designed to help local authorities meet the special needs of Commonwealth immigrants. These provisions, however, have met with increasing criticism. I recognise that with the increasing number of people whose families are of overseas origin but who were born here, and who therefore cannot be described as immigrants, these provisions are ill-suited to our present times. We are now faced not so much with difficulties of newness, although these still exist, as with special problems of racial disadvantage arising particularly from colour and different cultural backgrounds. The Government has decided therefore that the existing statutory provisions need to be replaced. Accordingly this document presents some new proposals for helping those concerned to overcome problems of racial disadvantage.

However, to date, *Section 11 of the Local Government Act 1966* has not been replaced.

(ii) The Department of Education and Science

The Department of Education and Science is concerned with the Educational Priority Areas (1967), the Education Disadvantage Unit (1974) and the Centre for Information and Advice on Educational Disadvantage (1975). Following publication of the Plowden Report in 1967, which recommended that schools in deprived areas should be brought up to the standard of the rest of the country, £16 million was allocated over two years for a special building programme to replace old and unsatisfactory school buildings. In 1968, it was announced that teachers working in what were designated Educational Priority Areas should be eligible for a social priority allowance of £75 p.a. This was subsequently increased to £276. The Department of Education and Science also commissioned Dr A. H. Halsey to direct a number of action research projects in selected EPAs, the aim being to discover the most practical and effective ways of improving the education of children living in deprived areas. Five separate reports have been published, although some of their recommendations and conclusions are at variance with one another. One recommendation was that the years before children begin formal education are those in which schools can intervene most effectively in children's education. Apart from the education advantages of attending some form of nursery school, pre-school provision is of particular value to the children of working mothers, many of whom are forced to rely on childminders. Among these, women of West Indian origin feature prominently. However, in the last five years, public expenditure on nursery education has been subject to particularly serious cutbacks.

The Educational Disadvantage Unit was established in 1974 to act as a focal point for the exchange of advice and information between central and local government and others on measures to be taken to combat the effects of disadvantage and to influence the allocation of resources in favour of those areas which children were suffering from educational disadvantage. The Unit has established the Centre for Information and Advice on Educational Disadvantage (CIAED) and has organised a national conference and a series of seminars. The CIAED was established in 1975 to provide an information service and carry out a number of special inquiries. It subsequently decided that one of its special inquiries would be concerned with the educational needs of West Indian communities.

(iii) The Department of the Environment
The Department of the Environment has been responsible for Housing Action Areas and the Inner Area Studies, out of which developed *Policy for the Inner Cities*.[13] In 1977 the responsibility for the Urban Programme was transferred to this Department. In 1972 the Department of the Environment initiated studies of six urban areas with the aim of developing a more comprehensive approach to the improvement of the environment. The studies were intended to provide guidance to local authorities and were undertaken by consultants in collaboration with selected authorities under the direction of a Department of the Environment Steering Committee.

The reports of the first three studies were published in 1973. The other three studies were of districts in Birmingham, Liverpool and London which were defined as being typical of the 'inner city' and were published in 1977. These three areas contain a substantial number of black people and so the studies included some analysis of the socioeconomic position of black people. The general theme of the studies was that urban renewal is economically as well as socially a better alternative than further neglect. As part of a programme of renewal they recommended the creation of more employment and training opportunities for the unskilled and the unemployed. If successfully implemented, such a recommendation should benefit both black and white residents of such areas.

The Labour government's response to the Inner Area Studies was put forward in a White Paper, *Policy for the Inner Cities*, in June 1977. It defined four dimensions to the problem of the 'inner city': economic decline, physical decay (particularly of the housing stock), social disadvantage and the presence of 'ethnic minorities'. A commitment to arrest the decline of the 'inner city' is stated. The means to achieve this had an equally familiar ring about them. The Government proposed to give existing policies and programmes a special 'inner city' dimension, to strengthen the economies of these areas by means of existing industrial and employment policies (e.g. regional development policy, Industrial Development Certificates, Location of Offices Bureau, etc.), to encourage a unified approach to urban problems and to reorganise the Urban Programme. In order to encourage a unified approach to urban problems, the Government proposed to work in partnership with certain cities to develop inner area programmes. Concerning the Urban Programme, responsibility for it was transferred from the Home Office to the Department of the Environment, as was responsibility for the Comprehensive Community Programmes. Additionally, it was to be extended to cover industrial, environmental and recreational provision as well as social projects, and to increase expenditure to £125 million a year. As far as black people were concerned, it was stated that as they experienced the same disadvantage as other people living in these areas 'they should benefit directly through measures taken to improve conditions, for example, in housing, education and jobs. . . . However, the attack on the specific problem of racial discrimination and the resultant disadvantages must be primarily through the new anti-discrimination legislation and work of the Commission for Racial Equality.'[14] The *Inner Urban Areas Act* was passed in 1978 and nine Partnership and fifteen Programme Authority arrangements have since been established.

Finally, reference must be made to Housing Action Areas, which were established by the *Housing Act 1974*. A Housing Action Area was defined as an area where physical and social factors combine to create housing stress. Physical factors were to be assessed according to the proportion of houses lacking standard amenities, as well as those which are unfit for habitation. The social factors suggested relate to households sharing facilities, living in overcrowded conditions, with unsatisfactory tenure (generally in privately rented accommodation) and the incidence of households likely to have special housing problems (e.g. the special needs of the elderly). Local authorities were given greater powers of compulsory purchase and of compelling improvements from absentee landlords and were allowed to offer improvement grants of 75% to owner-occupiers and landlords; in cases of financial hardship this could be increased to 90%. The government committed itself to reimbursing 90% of local authorities' costs. As far as black people live in such accommodation (see Chapter 4) and as far as this accommodation is located in areas declared to be Housing Action Areas, one would expect them to benefit from this policy.

This brief survey of government urban and education policy gives rise to the following comments. First, there is evidence of a lack of general co-ordination. Different departments have initiated similar sorts of research and action and only since 1977 has there been anything approaching a 'co-ordinated' strategy to deal with the problem so regularly and clearly defined by different research projects. Second, the amount of money allocated to the various proposals and policies has been very small: about £121 million was committed by central government over the nine years from 1966 to 1975 to deal with urban and educational disadvantage. Given the scale of the problem, the increased expenditure announced in 1977 is still minute. Third, and following from the previous two points, there is no clear evidence of success. This is evident not only in the fact that governments over the past 12 years have regularly committed themselves to 'arresting the decline', thereby testifying to the fact that the previous effort did not achieve the aim, but also in that there is no study detailing the specific effectiveness of the money that has been spent. The latter point is of particular interest because successive governments have claimed that as black people share the economic and social disadvantages of urban decline with others living in the same areas, then action to eradicate those disadvantages will benefit everyone equally. As yet we have no hard evidence to show to what extent *anyone* has benefited from the policies described. Moreover, in the absence of evidence to the contrary, there is good reason to believe that black communities will not benefit equally from these policies just because of the nature and extent of racial discrimination.[15] For example, it is of little value to an unemployed black youth living in the inner city to provide special training when, once equipped with new skills, he/she is prevented from gaining a job because of racial discrimination in hiring practices. Moreover, a successful strategy for the inner city will require sensitive treatment of the needs and wishes of all the communities who live there.

Notes

1. This section does not aim to present a completely comprehensive account of the law relating to immigration control. The law in this, as in other areas, is very complex. The reader who wishes specific information relating to a specific case should obtain advice from a specialised agency. The intention here is to sketch out the main provisions of an Act of Parliament and to identify the main drift and underlying assumptions of the legislation.
2. C. Peach, *West Indian Migration to Britain* (London: Oxford University Press, 1968).
3. D. Hiro, *Black British, White British* (Harmondsworth: Penguin, 1971, pp. 209–10).
4. R. Moore and T. Wallace, *Slamming the Door* (London: Martin Robertson, 1975).
5. *Racial Discrimination*, Cmnd 6234, HMSO, 1975.
6. Ibid.
7. Ibid, para 50, HMSO, 1975.
8. *Review of the Race Relations Act 1976* (London: Runnymede Trust, 1979).
9. *Racial Discrimination*, Cmnd 6234, HMSO, 1975.
10. *Policy for the Inner Cities*, Cmnd 6845, HMSO, 1977.
11. C. Demuth, *Government Initiatives on Urban Deprivation* (London: Runnymede Trust, 1977).
12. Community Relations Commission Working Party, *Funding Multiracial Education: A National Strategy* (London: Community Relations Commission, 1976).
13. *Policy for the Inner City*, Cmnd 6845, HMSO, 1977.
14. *Policy for the Inner City*, Cmnd 6845, HMSO, 1977, p. 4.
15. C. Cross, *Ethnic Minorities in the Inner City* (London: Commission for Racial Equality, 1978).

3 Employment

In 1978 the labour force of Britain was 26 million people. According to the last census in 1971 a total of 1.5 million of the workforce were born outside the UK or had both parents born outside the UK. Approximately 0.5 million of these people were black. The patterns of employment – and indeed unemployment – amongst this black population differ in important respects from those of the British population as a whole. For example, proportionately more black people than white people have unskilled or semi-skilled jobs and the rate of unemployment for black youths is higher than that of their white peers.

These differences are a result of a number of factors which will be discussed in this chapter. Some are caused by racial discrimination; others are a consequence of some people from the Indian sub-continent having not been resident in the UK long enough to acquire the skills and language needed for work. Another factor is that the average age of the black population is much younger than the population as a whole. As young people are generally more likely to be unemployed (or take longer to enter into jobs), even without racial discrimination, unemployment rates for blacks, all other things being equal, would be higher than those for the population as a whole. For these and other reasons the black population is more susceptible to the effects of economic decline than the population as a whole. When unemployment rates rise, the black population is usually the first to suffer.

In Chapter 3 we discuss the occupational distribution of black people and the initiatives that have been taken to combat the discrimination and unemployment that black people face.

Black people in the working population
Black people form a relatively small but growing proportion of the

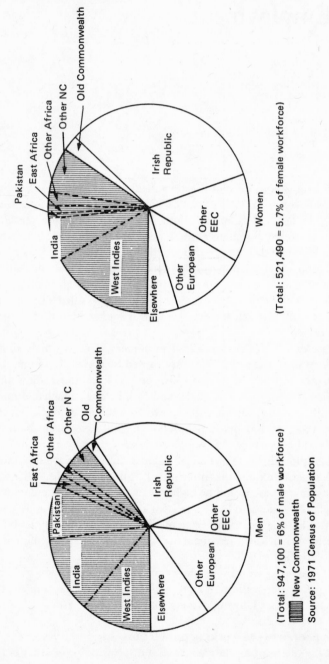

(Total: 947,100 = 6% of male workforce)

(Total: 521,490 = 5.7% of female workforce)

▤ New Commonwealth

Source: 1971 Census of Population

Fig. 3.1 Immigrant contribution to the labour supply, 1971.

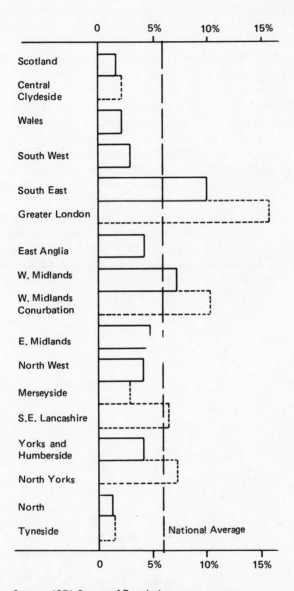

Fig. 3.2 Geographical distribution of immigrant workers, 1971. Economically active persons born outside UK and with both parents born outside UK as percentage of total economically active in region and conurbation.

labour force in Britain. In 1971, people who were born outside the UK or who had both parents born outside the UK accounted for just under 6% of all economically active persons: 2.2% (555,520) were from the New Commonwealth, 1.7% (421,130) from Ireland, and 2% from elsewhere. The figures are shown in Fig. 3.1.

The percentage of immigrants in the workforce varies from 1.3% in the North to over 15% in Greater London (this is shown in Fig. 3.2). Black people as immigrants settled in the more prosperous conurbations where their labour was in demand. In these conurbations they are often concentrated in inner city areas whose white and total population are declining. In these areas the demand for labour has been relatively high. However, in some cities there has also been a trend of population dispersal into the suburbs.

One study has shown that while the number of employed persons born in the UK fell between 1961 and 1971, the number of employed people born outside the UK rose (Fig. 3.3).[1] The increase in the number of economically active persons born in the New Commonwealth is likely to have continued for at least two reasons. First, children who came here to join their parents will have or will be reaching working age. Second, economically active immigrant males

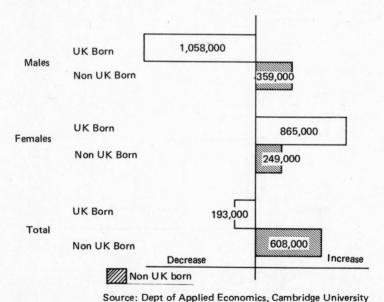

Source: Dept of Applied Economics, Cambridge University

Fig. 3.3   Changes in numbers employed, 1961–1971.

from the New Commonwealth have a lower average age than that for economically active males taken as a whole. Comparisons between blacks and whites are strongly influenced by the difference in age profile – a far greater percentage of whites than of blacks are above retiring age. Because of this, a relatively high proportion of men from the black groups are working – 91% of black men in comparison with 77% of white men. In 1971 half the number of black women aged 15 and over were economically active, compared with 43% of women for the general population.

There were, however, marked differences between activity rates of the different groups that comprise the black population. For example, 67% of West Indian women aged 15 and over were economically active in contrast to only 39% for Indian women and 16% for Pakistani women. It is likely that the religious and cultural pressures on women from the Indian sub-continent (especially Pakistani women, who are mainly Moslems) not to seek employment outside the home will relax, to some extent. This is particularly likely if 'ethnic work groups' can be established so that women can work together with no direct contact with men.

Black people work in a wide range of mainly manual industries and occupations but tend to be concentrated in unskilled and semi-skilled jobs for which it is difficult to recruit or retain workers because of 'unsocial' hours, an unpleasant working environment and relatively low earnings. Reasons for this include language difficulties and differences in educational and training standards which are not readily acceptable to British employers. Moreover, it should be remembered that these features characterised those sectors of the economy that were short of labour in the late 1950s and early 1960s, this shortage being the initial stimulus for immigration. Hence, black people work in these industries and occupations partly because these were the ones which were willing to employ them. But it is also the case that movement out of these industries and occupations is retarded by racial discrimination.

The proportion of those in each industry in 1971 who were immigrants are shown in Fig. 3.4. Of all employed immigrants 36% of all employed immigrants and 47% of those from the New Commonwealth worked in manufacturing industries III to XIX (see Fig. 3.4). The corresponding percentage of all employed persons was 33%. A number of studies have indicated that home-working, often with very low wages, is widespread amongst women from the Indian sub-continent and from Cyprus.[2] West Indian women seem

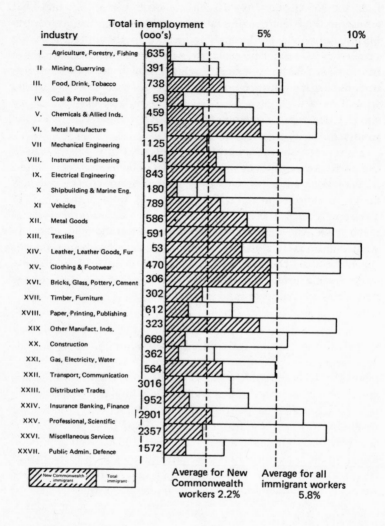

Fig. 3.4 Immigrant workers as a percentage of the total workforce by industry.

more likely to work outside the home. This difference is explained by the language and cultural barriers which prevent many Asian women from taking a job outside the home.

According to the 1971 Census a much higher proportion of economically active black people than of the population as a whole were labourers and the proportion of black people who were administrators and managers, clerical or sales workers, was well below the corresponding proportion for all economically active persons. In the manufacturing industries, black people generally worked directly in production or related activities such as packing and relatively few in service or maintenance. Black workers are greatly underrepresented at supervisory levels. According to a recent report, employers largely attributed this to a combination of low turnover among existing supervisors and promotion systems which depend largely on seniority coupled with the presence within the organisation of white workers with greater seniority than any black employees.[3]

Black people are more likely to be employed on shifts, particularly night shifts. The PEP study showed that 32% of the plants visited in which members of the ethnic minorities accounted for most of the workforce had permanent night shifts as compared with only 12% of those firms employing only white workers (see Fig. 3.5).[4]

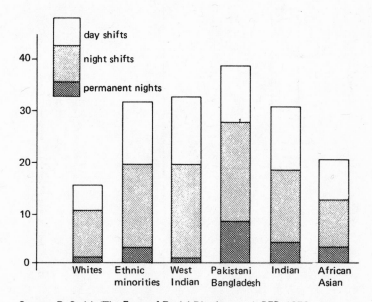

Source: D. Smith 'The Facts of Racial Disadvantage': PEP, 1976

Fig. 3.5   Percentage of male workers working shifts (by country of origin).

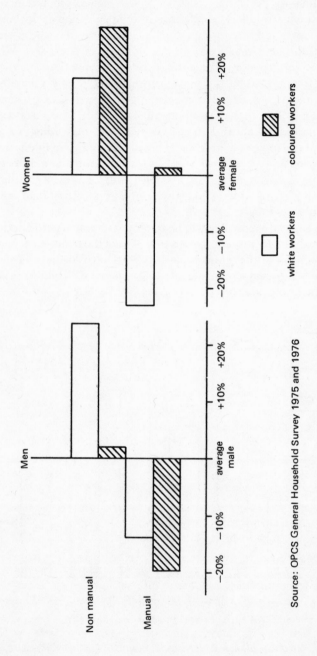

Source: OPCS General Household Survey 1975 and 1976

Fig. 3.6 Comparison of average earnings for white and coloured workers against overall average for sex.

As is shown in Fig. 3.6, both manual and non-manual black male workers are likely to earn less than white workers. However, because there are fewer part-time workers in the black female earning group than in the white female earning group, the earnings of black women will tend to be higher than those of their white counterparts although pay rates may be lower. These differences in earnings are attributable to the fact that black workers tend to be concentrated in lower status jobs and those with less responsibility.

In London a high proportion of West Indians are in transport and labouring jobs, while in the West Midlands many black people and especially Pakistanis are in labouring jobs. Indians in the West Midlands are disproportionately represented in furnace, forge, foundry and rolling mills. In the London area Cypriots and Pakistanis are concentrated in service occupations and in the clothing trades.

Another study showed that the pattern revealed by PEP at a national level was reflected in a typical West Midlands town.[5] In a sample of firms which together employed some 1800 black people most black employees were shown to be employed in unskilled or semi-skilled jobs. Most firms only recruited black workers because no suitable whites were available, and of the 1800 black workers in the sample only two were foremen.

Although immigrant labour accounts for only about 6% of all economically active persons in Britain, it forms a sizeable element in the labour force of certain firms and industries. Examples include

1.   Textiles in Lancashire and Yorkshire where nightshifts are often manned almost entirely by Indian and Pakistani workers;
2.   The National Health Service in England and Wales in which over one-third of hospital medical staff, about one-sixth of doctors in general practice and a little over one-fifth of all student and pupil nurses and pupil midwives are born overseas;[6] and
3.   Restaurants, cafes and snack bars in which nearly one-quarter of all workers nationally and over one-half in Greater London are immigrants.

Discrimination in employment

There is evidence from a number of reports and surveys of widespread discrimination against black people in British industry. One report suggests that discrimination is not a question of employers simply displaying prejudice against people with black skins, but that employers appear to have mistaken assumptions about the actual abilities of black people.[7]

A survey of nearly 300 plants, comprising case studies and interviews conducted by PEP, showed that more than half the plants practised some form of discrimination and a black person had to make twice as many applications as a white person before finding a job.[8] A second PEP report[9] in the same year stated that substantial discrimination was found, even at the level of recruitment for unskilled jobs; further, more than 30% of Indian and West Indian applicants were discriminated against at the earliest stage of recruitment – the written application stage – in a broad range of white collar jobs. This research included Greek subjects to test the extent to which discrimination related to 'foreigness' rather than skin colour. Its authors stated that the findings in all the tests strengthened the conclusion that it was skin colour which underlay most of the discrimination shown in these cases.[9]

According to a report published by the Tavistock Institute of Human Relations, black people are considerably less successful than whites in applying for jobs and promotion in the Civil Service.[10] The departments studied were the Department of Health and Social Security, the Ministry of Defence and H.M. Dockyard, Portsmouth. In the London North DHSS Region, out of 317 applications for clerical officer grade jobs between June and November 1976, one-third came from black candidates and two-thirds from whites. Only ten black candidates were offered jobs in comparison with 78 whites: this translates to a success rate of 18% in comparison with 54% for whites. Furthermore, more black than white candidates rejected for interview possessed the minimum educational qualifications. The researchers also found that of 100 clerical officers studied, 30 were 'over-qualified' and of these 23 were black, showing that many black employees accept jobs below their level of qualification.

Unemployment

In February 1980, according to figures published by the Department of Employment, there were 1422.0 thousand persons (or 6.0% of the total workforce) unemployed in Great Britain. Of these, 54.4 thousand were black.[11] Unemployment amongst black people, as a percentage of all those registered as unemployed in the UK, has increased rapidly during the past few years. This is shown in Fig. 3.7. There is, however, evidence to suggest that this is primarily a

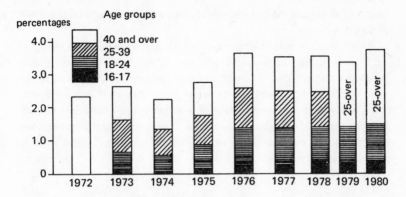

Source: Department of Employment, *Gazette*, 1980, Vol. 88(3).

Fig. 3.7   Unemployment among minority groups as a percentage of total unemployed.

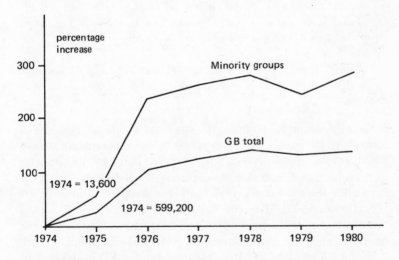

Source: Same as for fig. 3.7.

Fig. 3.8   Percentage increase in unemployment since 1974 of minority groups and total workforce in Great Britain.

result of the rapid rise in unemployment amongst black youths aged from 16 to 24.

According to both Department of Employment figures and the PEP survey, unemployment among black people increases disproportionately when the general level of unemployment is rising (see Fig. 3.8). For example, between November 1973 and February 1980 total unemployment doubled, whereas the number of black people on the register quadrupled. Several factors have been suggested to explain why unemployment among black people increases in this way:

1. There are increasing numbers of black young people leaving full-time education and entering the employment field at a time when job prospects for young people generally are adversely affected by the cutbacks in recruitment during the present recession.
2. The shorter average duration in employment of black workers makes them vulnerable to 'last in, first out' rule at times of redundancy.
3. There have been greater percentage increases in unemployment in the regions – for example, the South East and West Midlands – where most black people live.
4. Racial discrimination by individual employers and in recruitment and selection procedures means that, faced with a plentiful supply of labour, employers will hire white in preference to black labour.
5. Lack of appropriate skills and qualifications including knowledge of English on the part of recent immigrants from the Indian subcontinent.

How important each of these factors is relative to all the others is difficult to determine. Without doubt, given the evidence on the extent of discrimination which occurs when black people apply for jobs, racial discrimination is a major factor, but it does not necessarily follow that the other factors are of only peripheral importance.

Statistics published by the Department of Employment showed that between February 1979 and February 1980 registered unemployment among black workers rose by 11.6% compared with 2.5% for the total unemployed for Great Britain.[12] The increase was not evenly spread through the black workforce. Among West Indians, unemployment went up by 13.5% while among Pakistanis it increased by 10.1%. There does not appear to be a single explanation for those discrepancies, and it would seem that differing industrial occupation, area of residence and age structure may all have been contributory factors.

Youth unemployment

In general, black school-leavers are particularly likely to be unemployed. This is both because of a reduction in the number of jobs available and because the black population is on average younger than the population as a whole, so even without discrimination proportionally more blacks than whites would be unemployed.[13]

Between February 1977 and February 1978 the increase in unemployment in the 16–24 age group accounted for 36% of the total increase in unemployment for Asian workers (excluding those from East Africa). Between February 1979 and February 1980, unemployment amongst black youths increased by the same percentage (11%) as for the total black unemployed. Allowing for a low level of registration (see below), particularly among young people, these figures are probably a considerable underestimate of unemployment among young black workers.

Unregistered unemployment

The number of people who are unemployed but have not registered as such at employment offices and jobcentres is by definition difficult to assess. The Department of Employment estimated that in 1973 there were a total of 100,000 unregistered males and 160,000 unregistered females.[14] The 1971 Census showed that the *majority* of unemployed black people were not registered as unemployed in 1971. This may be for a number of reasons including the fact that some black people may be disenchanted with the kinds of jobs thought to be suitable and therefore offered to them by local employment offices. The fact that just under half of the males born in the West Indies who were not working were not registered as unemployed meant that they were not eligible for benefits. More recent estimates of the extent of non-registration have varied[15] though it is probably true to say the level of non-registration amongst blacks, particularly young West Indians, is considerably higher than amongst the total population even within a similar age range.

According to a survey published in 1978, unemployment among black school-leavers in the borough of Lewisham in London is three times higher than among white school-leavers despite the fact that they try just as hard to find jobs.[16] Those in employment had taken longer to find work and have had to try harder than their white contemporaries. Both the black and white unemployed sample were actively looking for work and two-thirds of the unemployed blacks thought that they had been discriminated against by employers. Although the educational achievement of the black sample was on average lower, it did not seem to be a crucial factor in explaining the different success rates in finding jobs. The survey of 500 school-leavers concluded that 'whether intentional or unintentional' discrimination has been an important factor.

Responses to unemployment and discrimination
There have been a number of attempts to improve the position of black people in the employment field and to alleviate the problems of unemployment which they face particularly acutely. The most substantial government response has been in terms of employment and training programmes. It is difficult to gauge the effectiveness for these measures for black people because although it is possible to use figures on employment as some indication of need, few of the measures have been designed to alleviate unemployment amongst black people alone. The principal measure intended to help combat discrimination in employment is the *Race Relations Act 1976*. Although it is possible to gauge the extent to which the Act has been used, it is difficult to assess the extent of discrimination which is in fact taking place. Probably the most effective way of detecting discrimination, especially where it is of an indirect nature is to monitor the composition of the workforce of an organisation. Monitoring will be discussed more fully below.

Unemployment Government measures to alleviate unemployment have, to a certain extent, a special relevance for black people as they are particularly badly affected by Britain's present economic crisis. In March 1978 the programmes run by the Manpower Services Commission covered over 300,000 persons (at a time when the employment was about 1.3 million).[17] Over half of these people were employed through the Temporary Employment Subsidy by which the Government subsidised employers to take or keep on people they would otherwise not be able to afford to employ. Other schemes include a variety of training measures, Community Industry projects and Work Experience and Job Creation Programmes (JCP). In December 1978 JCPs were replaced by the Special Temporary Employment Programme (STEP) and the Youth Opportunities Programme (YOP). The total estimated cost of these programmes for 1978/9 is £695.7 million. The Manpower Services Commission stated that they recognise a special responsibility for groups liable to discrimination in finding jobs such as ethnic minorities.[18]

As unemployment is particularly high amongst school-leavers and young people, many of the Government unemployment programmes are directed towards them. As we have already seen, young blacks are even more likely to be unemployed than others of this age group. For this reason, certain government training schemes have been initiated so as to be of use to young blacks. One non-government project – the Fullemploy Training Scheme – has since 1976 run courses for young people to develop skills which will consequently allow them to gain relevant experience and thereby improve their employment prospects.[19] This particular scheme helped to place a small number of young West Indians in office jobs in the City of London.

The difficulties that black people face in employment are, how-ever, not as much a result of any lack of skills or abilities on their part as much as the circumstances with which they are confronted. A British Youth Council's report made the following comment: 'Although many of the disadvantages suffered by ethnic minorities are the same as those suffered by other young unemployed people, all the available evidence points to racial discrimination as being the major factor in the disproportionately high youth unemployment levels they face.'[20]

Discrimination Employment is one of the areas covered by the *Race Relations Act 1976* (see Chapter 2). In the twelve months between September 1977 and September 1978 a total of 524 complaints of racial discrimination were made to industrial tribunals. Between the Act coming into force on 13 June 1977 and March 1979 there had been 33 successful complaints to industrial tribunals. In most cases compensation is only given for injury to feelings and the sum involved rarely exceeds £100.[21] Also under the Act the CRE is empowered to conduct formal investigations into the practices of employers as well as other organisations. In the first 18 months of the operation of the Act 22 formal investigations has been initiated by the CRE, a majority of which concerns employment. The National Bus Com-pany, Chubb and Son Ltd, Unigate and the Prestige Group are amongst those who have been investigated. At the conclusion of an investigation, the CRE may issue a non-discrimination notice which requires the individual or organisation to stop the practice of discri-mination. The first non-discrimination notice was issued in November 1978 to a restaurant and disco called Pollyanna's in

Birmingham, where the management had repeatedly refused to cater for parties that included black people. It should be noted that th CRE has been criticised for not making the maximum strategic use of its powers of formal investigations.[22]

Another way in which the government can discourage discrimination is by using its power as an employer to ensure that those firms from which it contracts goods or services provide information on their employment practices concerning equal opportunities. *Racial Discrimination,* the White Paper which preceded the *Race Relations Act 1976,* had pledged that the government would take a more active role in reducing discrimination in employment. The plans which were announced on 1 November 1978 included the Department of Employment's intention to request information to determine whether a contractor's practices are in compliance with the Act and to see what steps are being taken to avoid direct and indirect discrimination. Cases where there were serious doubts regarding the contractor's compliance with the law are to be referred to the Commission for Racial Equality.[23]

Monitoring and equal opportunity There are two ways of identifying whether racial discrimination is occurring within a workplace. The first is to survey complaints of discrimination made at industrial tribunals. The second is to monitor the recruitment and promotion of black employees in relation to the rest of the workforce.[24]The Tavistock Report, discussed above, is an example of this second approach.[25]

As a positive response to the difficulties faced by black people in employment there have been a number of moves designed to ensure equal opportunities. The CRE has encouraged employers to publish and adopt equal opportunity policies.[26] By 1979 over 50 companies ranging in size from small employers to nationalised industries had adopted equal opportunity policies many of which included monitoring. A policy, is of course effective in itself, but such a statement of intent can be helpful because it often leads to action to eliminate discriminatory practices.

The Institute of Personnel Management has made an initial move to come to terms with the development and maintenance of non-discriminatory selection tests.[27] Training courses and programmes for black workers can also play a part in promoting equal opportunity by allowing employees to make maximum use of their abilities. One barrier to this development, especially for recent immigrants from the Indian sub-continent, can be the lack of a good command of

English. The National Centre for Industrial Language Training (NCILT) specialises in developing and organising English Language training in the workplace. Since 1974 the Department of Education and Science has established 26 language training units based on the 'Pathway' scheme which took place in the London Borough of Ealing. Under these schemes language training is carried out at the place of employment.

As with education generally, training programmes for all an organisation's employees can also help to encourage equal opportunity by helping them to become aware of the cultural differences between minority groups. The Department of Employment has established a Race Relations Employment Advisory Service to help the employers with the management of a multi-ethnic workforce.

Despite its opposition in principle to racial discrimination, the Trades Union Congress (TUC) made no attempt before the mid 1970s to campaign actively against racism and racial discrimination within the ranks of the trade union movement or within the workplace. In recent years the Trades Union Congress has begun to make some effort to tackle some of these issues.[28] In 1975 the General Council of the TUC asked all affiliated unions to negotiate for equal opportunity clauses to be included in collective agreements. Also in 1975 the TUC set up an Equal Rights Committee with two advisory committees, one of which was the Race Relations Advisory Committee. More recently, after the violence in the East End of London in the summer of 1978, The South-East Regional Council of the TUC initiated a programme to improve trade union organisation amongst black workers in the East End and to encourage the development of equal opportunity policies.

Notes

1. Department of Applied Economics, Cambridge University. Referred to in *The Role of Immigrants in the Labour Market,* Runnymede Trust Briefing Paper, 1977.
2. S. Shah, *Immigrants and Employment in the Clothing Industry: the rag trade in London's East End* (London: Runnymede Trust, 1975).
3. Unit of Manpower Studies, *The Role of Immigrants in the Labour Market* (London: Department of Employment, 1977).
4. D. J. Smith, *Racial Disadvantage in Employment* (London: Political and Economic Planning, 1974).
5. D. Brooks, *Black Employment in the Black County* (London: Runnymede Trust, 1975).
6. British Medical Association, 'Medical Manpower, Staffing and Training Requirements', *British Medical Association Journal*, 19 May 1979, pp 1365–76.
7. Unit of Manpower Studies, op. cit.
8. Smith, op. cit.

9. D. J. Smith and N. McIntosh, *The Extent of Racial Discrimination*, PEP vol. XI, Broadsheet 547, 1974.

10. Tavistock Institute of Human Relations, *Application of Race Relations Policy in the Civil Service* (London: HMSO, 1978).

11. Department of Employment, *Gazette*, March 1980, Vol. 88, no. 3, p. 245.

12. Department of Employment, *Gazette*, 1979, Vol. 87, no. 3, p. 259 and 1980, Vol. 88, no. 3, p. 245.

13. Youthaid, *Study of the Transition from School to Working Life*, London, 1979.

14. Department of Employment, *Gazette;* December 1976, Vol. 84, no. 12.

15. M. Navitt, *Unregistered Unemployment: a background paper* (London: Youthaid, 1979).

16. Commission for Racial Equality, *Looking for Work*, London, 1978.

17. Manpower Services Commission, *Review and Plan, 1977*, London, 1977.

18. M. A. Pearn and J. Munene, *Increasing Employability: an evaluation of the Fullemploy Training Scheme* (London: Runnymede Trust and the Manpower Services Commission Training Services Division, 1978).

19. British Youth Council, *Youth Unemployment: causes and cures*, London, 1977.

20. Runnymede Trust, *A Review of the Race Relations Act 1976*, London, 1979.

21. Ibid.

22. *Runnymede Trust Bulletin*, April 1979, no. 108.

23. Commission for Racial Equality, *Monitoring and Equal Opportunity Policy: a guide for employers*, London, 1978.

24. Tavistock Intitute of Human Relations, op. cit.

25. Commission for Racial Equality, op. cit.

26. Institute of Personnel Management, *Towards Fairer Selection: a code for non-discrimination*, London, 1978.

27. R. Miles and A. Phizacklea, 'The TUC, Black Workers and New Commonwealth Immigration, 1954–1973', *SSRC Working Papers on Ethnic Relations*, 1977, no. 6; R. Miles and A. Phizacklea, 'The TUC and Black Workers, 1974–1976', *British Journal of Industrial Relations*, 1978, Vol. XVI, pp. 268–78.

4 Housing

In Chapter 4 we look at the quality of accommodation in which Britain's black population live and also their access to council housing and other forms of tenancy. It is clear from a number of studies that West Indian and Asian people tend to live in lower standard housing than the rest of the population. Some of the factors that account for this are discussed below together with some of the moves that are being made to promote equal opportunities in the housing market for all people, irrespective of their colour.

Quality and tenure of housing

Since 1945 housing conditions in Britain have improved considerably. Nevertheless in 1977 over 8% of households still shared or lacked at least one of the three basic amenities, that is to say a fixed bath or shower, plumbed hot water and an inside WC.[1] It is clear that a greater proportion of black people live in housing with poor amenities than white people (see Fig. 4.1). Overcrowding can be assessed by setting a 'bedroom standard' of one bedroom per married couple, plus one per single adult, one per pair of older children of the same sex, and one per pair of younger children. Using this measure Fig. 4.1 shows that the proportion of overcrowded households is greater for black people than for white people.

Another measure of housing quality is the extent to which two or more households share their dwelling. Again the position of black people is worse than that of white people, but care must be taken with this measure because some people like sharing their house so that perhaps a measure of 'undesired sharing' would be more appropriate. Note how in all three charts the housing quality varies between black groups.

The quality of housing occupied by black people is, of course,

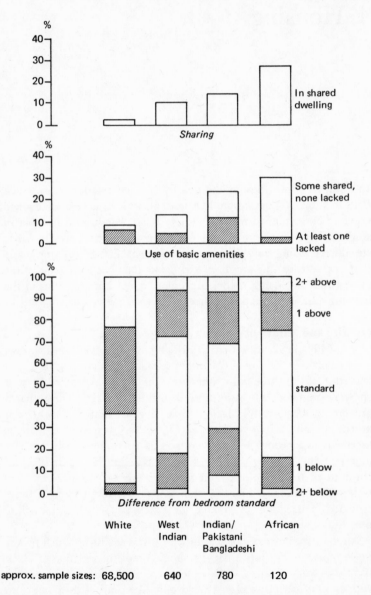

source: Dept. of Environment, National Dwelling & Housing Survey; HMSO, 1979, table 8.

Fig. 4.1 Housing quality by ethnic group of head of household.

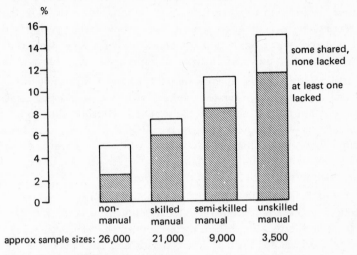

Fig. 4.2   Use of housing amenities by job type of head of household.

related closely to their general position in society. Housing quality, for example, is closely related to the socioeconomic group of the head of household. Fig. 4.2 shows how households with 'white collar' or skilled heads have on average better quality housing than those with manual workers or unskilled heads. Because black people tend to be in the 'lower' socioeconomic groups, which are also the least well paid, this explains to a certain extent their overall representation in poor quality housing.

A further explanation for black people's poor quality housing is that black immigrants, like previous immigrants such as the Jews, were forced because of their financial circumstances to take on property that other people were rejecting. Just as black immigrants were prepared to do the jobs which whites were not prepared to do, so they were prepared to take the housing that was not acceptable to whites. In certain circumstances, immigrants were willing to purchase apparently low-quality, short-lease property at very low prices because such action was in accordance with their intention of only a short-term stay in Britain.[2]

Very often this was located in the already declining inner areas of cities. In addition to these factors it is undoubtedly the case that direct racial discrimination against black people in the housing field, particularly before this was made unlawful by the *Race Relations Act 1968*, meant that only certain types of property was available to them.

It should be possible to use National Dwelling and Housing Survey (NDHS) data to investigate whether the factors mentioned above can explain all of black people's poorer housing situation, or whether, as was discovered in the large 1974 PEP survey, poor black people have worse housing than poor white people, and well-off black people worse housing than well-off white people (Tables B84 and B89 Smith (1976) not reproduced here).[3]

About 54% of the heads of households in Britain are owner-occupiers, 30% rent from their local council and 15% rent from private landlords.[4] Fig. 4.3, using data collected in 1978, shows that the proportions for West Indians, Asians and Africans differ from this, and from each other. A much larger proportion of Asians are borrowing money to buy their houses, and their use of council housing is only one-third of the national average. In contrast West Indians use council housing more than the average with very few owning their houses outright.

The situation is rapidly changing: council renting and house buying is increasing and private renting is decreasing. The PEP report gave the proportion of West Indian households in council housing as 26% and for Asians as 4% in comparison with the 1978 NDHS figures of 45% and 10%.[5]

The authors can think of no statistical reason why these differences should be found, and thus conclude that they are real. They may perhaps show that in the four years between the two surveys many of Britain's black people had lived in their local area long enough to satisfy the residence qualifications and to reach the top of the waiting list for council houses. Some may also have benefited from slum clearance programmes.

Fig. 4.4 shows the breakdown of tenure by social class for the general population, West Indian and Asians. In the general population, the 'higher' the social class the more owner-occupiers and the less council tenants there are. The West Indian population has a relatively similar council tenancy between social classes, owner-occupation replacing private renting the 'higher' the social class. For the Asian population, there appears to be less owner-occupation

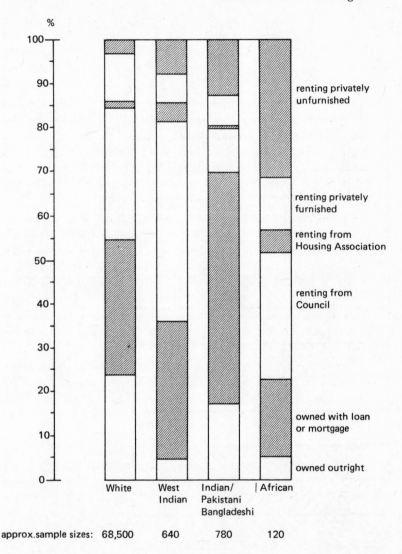

%

renting privately
unfurnished

renting privately
furnished

renting from
Housing Association

renting from
Council

owned with loan
or mortgage

owned outright

White   West   Indian/ | African
         Indian   Pakistani
                  Bangladeshi

approx.sample sizes: 68,500   640   780   120

source: Same as fig. 4.1.

Fig. 4.3   Ethnic group of head of household by tenure.

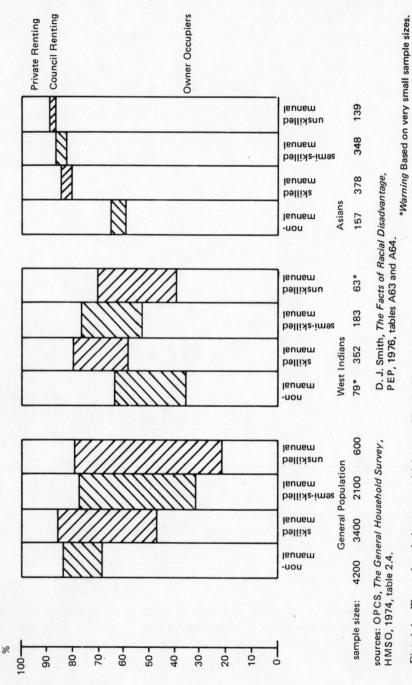

sources: OPCS, *The General Household Survey*,
HMSO, 1974, table 2.4.

D. J. Smith, *The Facts of Racial Disadvantage*,
PEP, 1976, tables A63 and A64.

Warning Based on very small sample sizes.

Fig. 4.4   Tenure by ethnic group and job type of head of household.

amongst the 'higher' social classes. However, these differences have to be treated with caution because they are based on small sample sizes.[6]

If socioeconomic group can be used as a proxy for economic class, and if council housing is for the poor, it can be seen that, contrary to claims that 'they' take up all 'our' council houses, neither West Indians nor Asians are occupying council housing in as large a proportion as are similar members of the population as a whole.

Home Ownership: The financing of owner-occupation

Another disadvantage black people face is in the difficulty they experience in obtaining loans to buy their own house. Again it can be shown that the differences are only partly accounted for by the fact that black people are generally poorer than whites and thus in a worse position to make the best choice.

Table 4.1 is based on Valerie Karns' study of three inner city areas of Birmingham.[7] In it the differences in the distribution of source of mortgage finance by applicant's place of birth are compared with national figures for the period 1972–4. There were too few West Indians in the sample to draw any meaningful conclusions so the next paragraph looks at Asians and whites only.

The policy of some building societies of 'red-lining' (that is not allowing mortgages on houses in specified inner city areas, regardless of the quality of the houses or the credit-worthiness of the mortgage applicant) has affected all buyers, not just blacks. Because of this common practice whites often turn to the local council for a mortgage while most Asians seek a bank loan, which is usually much faster to obtain but involves paying much higher interest rates. White people complain that by the time they have arranged a mortgage advance to purchase a house it has been bought by an Asian family with cash. Table 4.1 shows that they proabably did not have cash as such but had arranged a bank loan, a procedure which takes less time to process than the conventional mortgage application. This often forces other families to seek bank loans too. If local authorities could speed up their loaning procedures, or if building societies became more willing to lend money on housing needing improvement (as much of housing in these areas does) – perhaps conditional on improvement work being carried out within a specified period – then the money now spent on exorbitant interest payments to banks could be spent instead of improving basically good housing.

Table 4.1   Main source of finance for house buying by country of birth

From a survey of people buying houses in three inner city areas of Birmingham 1972–4

Source of finance	Britain and Ireland (%)	Pakistan/ Bangladesh (%)	India (%)	Comparative national figures (%)
Local authority	16	3	16	9
Building society or insurance company	37	3	5	85
Bank	10	63	41	
Fringe bank/finance company	11	11	9 ⎫	
Vendor/solicitor	3	1	2 ⎬	6
Friend/relative	—	3	5 ⎭	
Cash	23	15	20	
No reply	1	—	2	
Sample sizes	111	155	93	

(*Source:* Karn 'The financing of owner-occupation and its impact on ethnic minorities', 1977, Table 7.)

Council housing

In 1975 the Runnymede Trust published a report which used the small area statistics from the 1971 Census to show firstly that black people were underrepresented in council housing and secondly that the black tenants of the GLC were far more likely to be in pre-war flats in central London whereas white tenants were more likely to be in the newer cottage estates.[8] The GLC's eventual reply gave figures from a specially commissioned survey of their tenants which confirmed that this was indeed the case.[9] Tables 4.2 and 4.3 reproduced from the report show this clearly. The report went on, however, to show (see Table 4.4) that much of this discrimination applied to other disadvantaged groups also. The reason black people did so badly was that so many of them were in these disadvantaged groups, though within any one such group the black tenants had on average worse housing than white tenants.

The GLC's explanation of these findings was not that discrimination had taken place, but that the allocation procedures were working against, rather than for, the disadvantaged and the black tenants. The homeless are in more urgent need of housing, therefore they tend to reject offers less often (indeed the procedures restrict the number of rejections they are allowed to make relative to other

Table 4.2   Area of London lived in by GLC tenants, by colour
From Greater London Council Lettings Survey 1975

	Inner London	Percentage of tenants in Outer London	Outside London	Sample sizes
White	62.5	24.2	13.3	488
Non-white	90.9	6.8	2.3	397

(*Source:* Parker and Dugmore, *Colour and the Allocation of GLC Housing: The Report of the GLC Letting Survey,* 1976, Table 4.4.)

Table 4.3   Type of estate lived in by GLC tenants, by colour
From Greater London Council Lettings Survey 1975

	General property	Post-1945 cottage	Percentage of tenants in Post-1945 flatted	1919–45 cottage	1919–45 flatted	Pre-1919 all types	Sample sizes
White	11.7	17.0	33.8	8.4	24.6	4.5	488
Non-white	8.8	2.3	32.2	1.8	51.4	3.5	397

(*Source:* Parker and Dugmore, *Colour and the Allocation of GLC Housing: The Report of the GLC Letting Survey,* 1976, Table 4.5.)

Table 4.4   Disadvantaged groups of GLC tenants, by quality of housing and colour
From Greater London Council Lettings Survey 1975

	Homeless	Unemployed	Unskilled	Female single parent	Head of household under 30	Overall sample
Average quality (measured on an 8-point scale from 1 = post-1964 house to 8 = pre-1919 unmodernised flat)						
White	5.9	5.8	5.3	5.3	5.0	4.6
Non-white	6.2	6.2	6.4	6.0	5.9	5.8
Percentage in pre-1945 flats						
White	40	48	29	26	22	15
Non-white	52	56	57	53	52	44
Sample sizes						
White	73	25	63	42	148	469
Non-white	132	25	28	111	117	389

(*Source:* Parker and Dugmore, *Colour and the Allocation of GLC Housing: The Report of the GLC Letting Survey,* 1976, Table 5.19.)

prospective tenants) and so they are forced to take the more available but less desirable accommodation. In addition, housing managers, though denying that they purposely discriminate, do admit that in the interests of speed, white people are often not offered accommodation on estates which predominately house black people, or which are less desirable for some reason, because they assume they will refuse. The report destroyed the myth that black council tenants choose to congregate by showing that only about a half of GLC tenants (black or white) are allocated to their area of choice.

The London borough of Islington carried out a sample of its housing allocation to ethnic minorities which was published in 1977.[10] It found that 64% of UK and Irish nationals were allocated new accommodation compared with 41% of Cypriots, Europeans, and others of mixed origin and 30% of Africans, Asians, Caribbean and Chinese. Thus it can be seen that even within the public sector a market system is at work in which (as usual) the underdog fares worst. This seems to be the general pattern amongst local authorities. Several are realising the inadequacies of their points systems, and less discriminatory and more fair allocation systems are being advocated. The most comprehensive study on this subject is that by Smith and Whalley.[11] An interesting part of the GLC story is that the GLC needed specially to commission a survey to find out what colour their tenants were because this item of information was not kept in their records.

Location of housing

In Chapter 1 (Fig 1.5) we saw that Britain's black population is not evenly distributed through the whole country, but rather tends to be concentrated in many of the large cities in the major industrial areas. Within these cities again the black population is not evenly distributed but tends to be concentrated within particular boroughs or even wards. This can be shown using an index of segregation.[12] Table 4.5 shows this index calculated for wards in London for four groups (West Indians, Indians, Pakistanis and Irish) using 1971 Census data. The index would be 0 if a group were distributed amongst wards exactly like the overall population, and would be 100 if the group was wholly within one ward. The value of the index represents the percentage of the group who would have to move to make the distribution the same as the overall population. The table shows that concentrations were particularly high in 1971 for West Indians and Pakistanis.

The concentration of black homes in particular cities or specific districts has been an important consideration for those concerned with housing policy. Some of the issues involved were raised very acutely in the summer of 1978 over the GLC's decision to 'disperse' some three hundred Bengalis who had been living together in Spitalfields (see pp. 00–00). One point of view which has been taken for example by the Cullingworth report is that dispersal should be the aim, though not the overall preoccupation, of housing policy.[13] It has also been pointed out by Flett in a study of council housing in Birmingham that there is an important distinction to be made between spacial integration (that is geographical location) and social integration which encompasses social and economic position in society.[14] Also the interests of the tenants and those of the housing authority cannot always be assumed to be identical. It is perhaps only when a concentration of black people is automatically assumed to be a 'ghetto' that concentration is considered to be undesirable.

What *is* undesirable is for any particular group to be concentrated in poor quality housing in areas which lack social amenities. In a Department of Environment report it was shown that 10% of the census enumeration districts house 70% of the black population.[15] In these districts they comprise 20% of the total population. Also these districts contain three times as many households living at a density of over one and half people per room (the statutory over-crowding level).

What factors can account for this concentration of black people in certain areas of cities which are most often the poorest ones? Some segregation of groups of people is a consequence of the sort of jobs they do. For example, if a large proportion of manual workers live in certain areas of London and a large proportion of black people are manual workers, then obviously black people will tend to live in the same areas. Shah has calculated where the four groups he studied would live if their distribution amongst wards was entirely according to their occupation in the same way as the overall population. He then calculated the indices of segregation which there would have been and these are given in the second half of the Table 4.5.[16] It can be seen that for all groups the index drops dramatically, the extent of the drop representing that part of segregation *not* attributable to occupation thereby showing that most of the segregation of black people in London *cannot* be explained by their jobs.

In short, the evidence presented above shows that the economic position of Britain's black population is reflected in the location of their housing. Because they tend to occupy the bottom end of the labour market, black immigrants, like other immigrant groups before them, could only afford accommodation that was relatively inexpensive. This housing was therefore of a poorer quality and in less desirable areas. Thus the economic position in which black people are placed in British society forces an association between them and low standards of housing.

Table 4.5   Indexes of segregation of ethnic groups

	West Indians	Indians	Pakistanis	Irish
Index of segregation of actual distribution	52.2	38.9	54.9	29.1
Index of segregation of groups spread between wards by occupation class irrespective of ethnic group	8.5	1.3	5.1	5.1

Data based at ward level from 1971 population census for Greater London area.
(*Source:* Shah, *Some aspects of the Geographical Analysis of Immigrants in London*, 1978.)

The GLC and Bengali families in the East End
Last year the Greater London Council (GLC) announced a squatters' 'amnesty', under which those illegally in its property could register themselves and get the chance of being rehoused. The Bengali squatters (approximately 300 families) in Spitalfields are in housing the GLC wants to demolish and it would have to offer the Bengali families Council accommodation. The Bengalis, fearful of racialist attacks, requested to be housed in 'safe areas'. In addition, there was a regular demand from people who had been transferred to other parts of the borough to be returned to the Spitalfields area. The fear of racialist attacks was intensified last month when a young Bengali was stabbed (see Bulletin No. 99). On 4 June it was reported in the *Observer*, with the headline 'GLC Plans Ghetto for Bengalis', that the GLC was to earmark certain blocks of flats in or near Spitalfields for the exclusive use of Bengali families. It was reported that the decision, which was taken privately without reference to any committee, had the backing of both Labour and Tory leaders, and also met with the wishes of the Bengali Housing Action Group.

The following is a brief account of the controversy which followed:

5 June   It was reported in the *Guardian* that Mrs. Jean Tatham, chairman of the GLC Housing Committee, had stated that, 'the sensible thing seemed to be to distribute them around and break them up because we want to integrate these people if we possibly can. So despite all my good intentions it wasn't possible to do what I really would have preferred.' Mr. Horace Cutler, leader of the GLC, described the decision as 'a reasonable and sensible solution'.

8 June   It was reported in *The Times* that Mr. Alex Lyon MP had written to Sir Reg Goodwin, leader of the Labour group on the GLC, that the decision to set up a 'ghetto' posed a danger that racial groups would be sent to separate areas against their wishes. He said that, 'everyone, black or white, should be free to choose where to live'.

11 June   A report in the *Observer* said that Mrs. Jean Tatham had said that the setting aside of some blocks of flats in Spitalfields for Bangladeshi families was not her original intention; she had intended to authorise earmarking for the Bengalis only of vacancies in certain blocks, and not whole blocks. She was reported to have said that she was prepared to consider applications from all white groups who wanted to live separately on their own estates. Mr. Horace Cutler dismissed any suggestion of setting aside all-white estates. However, he agreed with the original decision to reserve certain blocks for the Bengalis in 'this one-off, no-win situation'.

The GLC's decision was attacked by Spitalfields Friends and Neighbours, Spitalfields Bengali Action Group, the Bangladesh Youth Association, and Chicksand Community Action Group. Mrs. Mala Dhondey of the Bengali Housing Action Group said that: 'the GLC has gone beyond what we asked in a potentially dangerous way. Our stress has been for housing on safe estates, spread mainly around the E1 area. But we have never said that we want all-Asian estates'.

13 June   Mr. Peter Shore, Secretary of State for the Environment, following a meeting with Mr. Horace Cutler, issued a statement saying that, 'it would be wrong to earmark particular blocks or estates for the exclusive occupation of particular ethnic minorities. Mr. Cutler assured me first that each of the families will retain the opportunity to make a real choice as to the area in which they want to live, and also that it was not the GLC's intention to accommodate Bengalis in blocks or estates which are ethnically exclusive'.

At a public meeting in Spitalfields Mrs. Jean Tatham explained that newspaper reports stating that the GLC planned to set aside blocks of flats in Spitalfields area for Bengalis should not be believed. She assured the Bengali community that they would not be forced to move if they did not want to. However, she refused to withdraw an internal report which was drawn up as a GLC response to the housing problems of the Bengali families. (*The Times,* 14 June 1978).

From: *Runnymede Trust Bulletin No. 100*

Furthermore their concentration in the already rundown areas of British cities has meant that black people came to be seen as a cause for the decline of areas rather than the victims of it.[17] Slums and bad housing existed before black immigrants ever arrived and continue to exist at their worst in cities such as Glasgow where very few black people have settled.

The social position of black people in British society is also reflected in the location of housing owned predominantly by black people. The identification of black with lower standards has provided grounds for one of the often repeated prejudices of white people against black people moving into their street. Also, in instances where the tensions of a community in decline are expressed in racial terms, some immigrant groups are forced for their own safety and protection to make their homes not only in particular areas but also in 'safe' blocks of flats within them. In the case of the Bengali community in Spitalfields, London, this has meant that squatting in completely dilapidated housing with their compatriots is considered preferable to suffering the racial abuse, injury and danger to life and property which living on a predominantly white housing estate can often involve.

Housing: responses to disadvantage

So far we have demonstrated that the black population, in comparison with the population as a whole, is disadvantaged as regards both the quality of housing and access to council housing. Two types of positive response to these facts can be distinguished. One seeks to improve housing conditions generally and thus improve the position of black people among others. The other seeks to improve the position of black people in the housing market both by attempting to cater for their particular needs and by attempting to remove the procedures which discriminate against them.

Here we shall consider official responses which have been concerned specifically with housing. However, as both the black population is concentrated within the inner areas of cities and the housing stock of these areas is of poor quality, then government policies directed towards reversing the decline of these areas, if successful, might be expected to improve the housing of black people in those areas. An outline of these policies is provided in Chapter 2.

General programmes and policies

The policy intention to provide help for black people through general improvements was expressed in the 1975 White Paper *Race Relations and Housing*.[18] Here the Government emphasised that the main contribution towards helping black people was to be made through general programmes and policies which had nothing to do with colour. More recently the 1977 consultative document *Housing Policy* states that black people will continue to benefit from policies designed to help those in housing need.[19] This document does, however, go on to recognise that black people face 'extra problems' in gaining access to local authority housing. These include the inability to meet residential qualifications and the size of families not matching the available accommodation (see below). Also in *Housing Policy* the government acknowledges that homelessness amongst young black people is an especially severe problem in some inner city areas. It suggests that the direct involvement of the black population – for example through self-help groups – is likely to achieve greater success than solutions imposed from above.

The housing conditions of black people will also be improved with the implementation of general programmes based on geographical areas. The higher level of grants from local authorities for home improvement and modernisation available to householders in Housing Action Areas are one example (see Chapter 2). As some of these schemes are located in the older housing districts of English cities where black people have been able to find accommodation they have stood to benefit from such general policies based on housing need. Some of the reasons for adopting a housing improvement policy and the issues that such a policy raised for a multi-racial area are discussed in the report of Oldham Community Development Project.[20]

Oldham Community Development Project. The following points are included in the summary of the report's findings:—

1. The white community of Glodwick identified immigrant groups (most notably Asian) as the most important source of the almost universally perceived decline of the area.
2. Racial negativism among white residents inhibits rehabilitation of the neighbourhood by its effect on mobility patterns and attitudes towards the area. In turn these affect the propensity of residents to invest in improvement.
3. Failure to invest reinforces processes of physical decline which in turn increase inter-ethnic tensions and bitterness. Unable to buy out of the area, poorer (and this usually means older) residents become 'trapped'.
4. The Asian community is increasing in numbers and is generally more satisfied and positive about an area. Increased numbers

and dissatisfaction with lower quality living environment exacerbate tensions.

5. Due to the disparity in attitudes between the white and Asian communities a free market process of race housing segregation is occurring. We believe this to be undesirable and recommend interventionist policies.

6. The major interventionist policy is housing improvement.

The redevelopment of an area by the building of new housing is another general method for improvement of housing stock. The benefits of such programmes for black people will again depend on their location and whether the black inhabitants of an area are rehoused in the same area once it has been redeveloped.

Discrimination

Racial discrimination on the part of those selling houses and those organisations involved in their finance, such as mortgage companies, have undoubtedly had the effect of limiting the choice of housing available to black people in both location and quality. Direct discrimination in housing was for the first time made unlawful in the *Race Relations Act 1968*. One of the most notorious convictions under the 1968 Act was that of Mr Robert Relf was was imprisoned in 1976 for contempt of court when he refused to remove a 'for sale to English only' sign from outside his home in Leamington Spa. During 1978 there were a total of 51 applications for assistance to the Commission for Racial Equality concerning housing: 21 were against local authorities, 19 against private landlords and 11 against estate agents.[21]

Perhaps of more importance than the discrimination against black individuals by white individuals is the discrimination, often of an indirect type, created through the 'normal' workings of many British institutions. Council housing unlike the private sector is under the control of a single authority in each area and provides an example of how institutional procedures and traditional methods of organisation often have the effect of discriminating against black people. This type of 'indirect discrimination' cannot be attributed to the personal feelings of the individuals who work in a particular organisation, but rather is part of the inherent structure of the organisation itself.

The *Race Relations Act 1976* made indirect discrimination unlawful. Moreover, local authorities' provision of council housing is one of the areas covered by Section 71 of this Act which states that:

It shall be the duty of every local authority to make appropriate arrangements with a view of securing that their various functions are carried out with due regard to the need:
a. to eliminate unlawful racial discrimination.

In addition the Act goes further to state that every local authority should also:

b. promote equality of opportunity and good race relations between persons of different racial groups.

A number of reports have made recommendations about how housing authorities can in practice fulfil their obligation under the *Race Relations Act 1976*. One produced by the Working Party of Housing Directors, made a series of recommendations for housing authorities in multi-ethnic areas.[22] These include providing interpreters and liaison staff for certain areas, training housing staff on the cultural background and family patterns of minority communities, ensuring minority representatives in residents' and tenants' associations and catering for the special needs of the different black communities such as single unemployed West Indian youth or the Asian elderly.

One of the more general points to be made from this is that equality cannot be guaranteed simply by treating everyone in the same manner. Unless a housing authority considers the differences in needs and circumstances of those on its housing list it will inevitably discriminate against certain groups. Thus in order to ensure equality the particular needs of black people must be taken into account together with those of other members of the community for whom the authority is responsible.

One approach towards ensuring that black people get their fair share of good quality council housing has been to set a target for allocating more desirable properties to black families. In January 1979 Lambeth council announced that a target proportion of 30% of the housing on new estates and modernised properties should go to black people on the waiting list.

The keeping of records on the ethnic origin of a council house tenants has for some time been advocated as an important means of working towards equality of treatment for all. Records can help to show whether housing procedures are working against black people. The recommendation to keep ethnic records was made by the Cullingworth Report in 1969.[23] This report suggested that local authorities should attempt to be colour conscious rather than 'colour-blind' because of the essentially discriminatory nature of housing management in that applicants are selected, assigned a priority and then allocated specific houses. More recently the London Housing Research Group has emphasised the value of keeping records and has made specific suggestions about the practical form such record-keeping should take.[24] Despite these endorsements the keeping of records is by no means common amongst housing authorities.

One of the main reasons for keeping records is that they can provide information – for example, to show how existing housing allocation procedures have the effect of not benefiting black people to the same extent as whites. As we have seen above, indirect discrimination means applying the same criteria to everyone with the effect that black people do not benefit as much as whites because of the essential characteristics of that criteria. One example of this is the residency requirement which until recently has been insisted upon by most housing authorities. This requirement means that housing applicants must have been resident in the area for a period before they can register on the housing list. Black people, particularly those from the Indian sub-continent, are less likely to be able to fulfil this requirement and therefore less likely to be offered council accommodation. The rule has provided the means for the discrimination.

Removal of this requirement can be seen as one of the positive steps to help achieve equality. In 1967 all London boroughs required a prior residential qualification: at that time 26 boroughs imposed a standard requirement of five years in London and one year in the borough.[25] In May 1975 the London borough of Hammersmith was the first to adopt a policy of rehousing applicants without any previous residence in the borough. By December 1977 this policy had also been adopted in the City of London and Havering and a further 11 boroughs had adopted less severe residence qualifications. The review of the first twelve months of the new policy in Hammersmith found that very little change in the size or composition of the waiting list had resulted but that a few cases of outstanding housing need had been helped more quickly.[26] As with other changes to help remove discrimination, there is a tendency for implementation to contribute to better management and use of resources overall.

Notes
1. Department of the Environment, *National Dwelling and Housing Survey* (London: HMSO, 1979).
2. D. Dahya, 'The nature of Pakistani ethnicity in industrial cities in Britain' in A. Cohen (ed.), *Urban Ethnicity* (London: Tavistock, 1974).
3. D. J. Smith, *The Facts of Racial Disadvantage* (London: Political and Economic Planning, 1976).
4. Department of the Environment, op. cit.
5. D. J. Smith, op. cit.
6. Office of Population Censuses and Surveys, *The General Household Survey* (London: HMSO, 1974).
7. V. Karn, 'The financing of owner-occupation and its impact on ethnic minorities', *New Community*, 1977/8, Vol. 6, nos. 1 and 2), pp. 49–64.
8. Runnymede Trust, *Race and Council Housing in London*, London, 1975.
9. J. Parker and K. Dugmore, *Colour and the Allocation of GLC Housing: The Report of the GLC Letting Survey, 1974–1975* (London: GLC, 1976).
10. London Borough of Islington, *Allocation of Islington Housing to Ethnic Minorities*, London, 1977.
11. D. J. Smith and A. Whalley, *Racial Minorities and Public Housing* (London: Political and Economic Planning, 1975).
12. S. Shah, *Some Aspects of the Geographical Analysis of Immigrants in London*, University of Oxford D.Phil. Thesis, 1978.
13. *Council Housing: Purposes, Procedures and Priorities* (London: HMSO, 1969).
14. H. Flett, 'Dispersal policies in council housing: arguments and evidence', *New Community*, 1979, Vol. 7, no. 2, pp. 184–94.
15. Department of the Environment, *Census Indicators of Urban Deprivation*, Working Note no. 8, London: 1976.
16. S. Shah, op. cit.
17. A. Phizacklea and R. Miles, 'Working class racist beliefs in the inner city' in R. Miles and A. Phizacklea (eds.), *Racism and Political Action in Britain* (London: Routledge and Kegan Paul, 1979).
18. *Race Relations and Housing*, Cmnd 6232 (London: HMSO, 1975).
19. *Housing policy: a consultative document*, Cmnd 6851 (London: HMSO, 1977).
20. A. Barr, *Housing Improvement and the Multi-Racial Community*, Oldham Community Development Project, 1978.
21. Commission for Racial Equality, *Annual Report, January–December 1978*, London, 1979.
22. Working Party of Housing Directors, *Housing in Multi-Racial Areas* (London: Community Relations Commission, 1976).
23. *Council Housing: Purposes, Procedures and Priorities*, op. cit.
24. Working Party of the London Housing Research Group, *Race and Local Authority Housing Information on Ethnic Groups* (London: Community Relations Commission, 1977).
25. Ibid.
26. London Borough Association, *Towards Ending Residential Qualification in London: A Report of a Working Group from the Association of London Borough Housing Officers*, 1977 (unpublished agenda item).

5 Education

There is little evidence to show that government or local authorities anticipated that changes might be required to the education system as a result of the entry into British schools of the children of immigrants coming to Britain to work. However, as we shall see in Chapter 5, these children were entering an education system which was organised on the assumption of cultural homogeneity and which was staffed by persons without any training which might prepare them to teach children either born outside Britain, or in Britain, of parents with a distinct culture. Moreover, the education system, in terms of both some of its staff and many of its books, has tended to reflect the racist ideology within British society which is, in part, a product of Britain's colonial and imperialist past. As these factors have played an important role in creating educational disadvantage amongst black children which is greater than that faced by white children in similar economic circumstances there is reason to be concerned.

Where and when recognition has been given to the implications of the entry of black children into British schools, it has often been defined as an 'immigrant' problem. This was and is inaccurate, not only because some 40% of the black population in Britain are British-born, but also because the problem lay not with the children but with a failure of the education system to respond quickly and intelligently to a new situation of cultural diversity which existed against the background of widespread racial discrimination. There are indeed very real problems arising from the fact that the school population includes children whose culture is quite distinct from each other: recognition of this has been slow and the amount of effort and time that has been spent in trying to solve these problems has been – and still is – small.

Statistics
The problem became defined in terms of 'immigrant' partly because statistics on the number of immigrant pupils were collected by the DES between 1966 and 1972. The decision to collect statistics on the

'immigrant' school population was justified on the grounds that the information was needed to arrange for the provision of language programmes. For these an 'immigrant' was defined as someone born outside the UK or born in the UK to parents who had been in this country for less than ten years. However, the statistics were not related to performance nor used to inform policy. In 1973 the Secretary of State for Education and Science stated: 'My department makes no use of them whatsoever except to publish them. They do not form the basis of any grant from my department . . . none of our grant formulae are on the basis of immigrants. . . .' (Mrs Margaret Thatcher, Secretary of State for Education and Science, June 1973). The DES discontinued the collection of these statistics and the Home Office has since relied on information from local authorities and will continue to do so until the collection of statistics is reintroduced. The Report of the *Select Committee on Race Relations and Immigration* on the West Indian Community in 1976 and the Green Paper *Education in Schools: A Consultative Document 1977* have stressed the need for statistical monitoring of pupils, students and teachers.

In 1971 Townsend and Brittan estimated that 3.3% of all pupils in maintained primary and secondary schools in England and Wales were immigrant pupils (their definition being based on the DES definition of 'immigrant'). More recent estimates of the size and distribution of the black school population have had to have been made indirectly, and the number of births to women born in the NCWP can be used as a rough guide to the size of the black school population. About 7% of all births are currently to women born in the NCWP. Since the black population is unevenly distributed around the country the proportion of black births to all births varies such that in some areas black children are not a small proportion of the school population but a significant element: this has serious implications for the authorities. Moreover while people of NCWP origin share the common label 'black', they come from different cultural backgrounds and thus have different experiences and needs.

The language issue

When black children first entered British schools, it was assumed that those in need would learn English through their interaction with other schoolchildren, but it became increasingly apparent that this was not happening and that extra language tuition was necessary. At this stage, it was assumed that the only children requiring such tuition were of Indian or Pakistani origin. West Indian children were perceived as having adequate command of the English language because of their having roots in a society which has an education system not only modelled on that of the English but also using English as the language of instruction. Accordingly, the language issue was defined as one of teaching English to mainly Asian children who had little or no command of the language.

Language tuition facilities have been provided since the early 1960s but there was and still is an acute shortage both of skilled teachers in English as a second language and of teaching materials. Townsend's study of local education authorities[1] showed that all 71 authorities made arrangements for the teaching of English at secondary level, all but four at the junior stage, and all but twelve at the infant stage.[2] However the provisions and facilities varied considerably and ranged from an extra teacher and a few lessons a week to full-time language classes within schools and a language centre. Moreover the scale of provision seemed to be closely related neither to the size of the black population nor to the extent of need.

The type of provision, size of the classes and the amount of tuition of English as a second language had also differed considerably. One of the first methods – and one which separated non-English speaking children least from the normal educational system – was called 'withdrawal' groups or classes. Another method is the 'part-time centre' to which non-English speaking children would be taken for half the day and then returned to school. This method has the disadvantage of interfering with the child's participation in normal school activities. Full-time language centres, separate from ordinary schools, have also been established. Perhaps the most satisfactory method is the specialised language-teaching department within an ordinary school. However, this requires specially trained teachers in English as a second language and there has always been a shortage of suitably qualified staff. The most common arrangement has been the 'reception classes' which were recommended in a Ministry of Education pamphlet *English for Immigrants* and in the Ministry's circular 7/65. This method has the advantage of combining intensive training without separation from the school, and in some schools the classes have grown into special English departments.

Much of the financial support for English teaching as a second language has come from Section 11 of the *Local Government Act 1966*. Education has in fact been the main user of this source of funds and has received roughly 80% of the funds which have been allocated. A report by the National Union of Teachers found that most of the grant was spent on teachers of English as a second language but that the take-up of the grant varied considerably amongst authorities and did not seem to be related to need.[3]

But teaching English as a second language requires more than just teaching staff: teaching materials are also required. In 1966 the 'Leeds Project' supported by the Schools Council produced teaching materials for children with an inadequate grasp of English: a similar project was started in Birmingham in 1967 to produce material for improving the language proficiency of West Indian children.[4] These initiatives were significant, for they marked the first move towards a serious consideration of the needs of black pupils. The shortage of teaching materials is still felt in spite of an increasing number of special schemes. The Centre for Urban Educational Studies is currently involved in a project which aims to provide teachers with the necessary skills for teaching English as a second language in primary schools. The Project's findings are being further developed on four parallel in-service courses, and the information is being incorporated into a book which will provide guidance on ways of working and some story packs. A Bilingual Education Project run by ILEA, which started in 1976, aims to produce a selection of learning materials in a variety of minority languages. They are intended for use by newly arrived secondary school age pupils whose knowledge of English is inadequate. A small selection of trial materials is already available.

Interest in and concern about the educational implications of West Indian children is a more recent development. Most West Indians in Britain, including those born in Britain, speak patois or Creole to some degree or another. Patois shares a large part of the vocabulary of English but is different in sound and grammar: accordingly some define it as a distinct language, but others see it as a dialect of English. Both in Britain and in the British Caribbean, West Indian speech varies along a patois–standard English continuum, the balance between the two being determined by the social situation. Edwards, amongst others, has argued that an increasing proportion of West Indian children in Britain, especially teenagers, are using a form of Jamaican patois much more exclusively as a response to their feelings of rejection and alienation.[5] However, it would be wrong to assume that only for these children is there a language issue in British schools. Edwards maintains from her and others' evidence that, because there is a continuum between standard English and patois, then there is a constant interplay or 'interference' between the two elements and that this places West Indian children in a disadvantageous position when educated through the medium of standard English. Disadvantage arises because teachers are commonly unsympathetic to the problems of comprehension and production of standard English faced by West Indian children, often to the extent that use of patois is believed to indicate low academic ability. There is then set in motion a cyclical process of low teacher expectation leading to low pupil performance.

As far as this issue has been recognised at all, the general response has been to attempt to force West Indian children to improve their standard English at the expense of patois. Edwards argues that this is unlikely to succeed and recommends the formal use of patois in British schools and the in-service training of all teachers who are likely to teach West Indian children so that they can recognise and encourage its use, at least in certain contexts. The Inner London Education Authority is attempting to encourage its teachers to develop a greater understanding of patois and to encourage its use in drama and poetry, an initiative which has met with opposition from teachers in some schools.

It is not clear whether the acceptance of the use of patois in schools will be encouraged by the EEC directive that member governments 'promote, in co-ordination with normal education, teaching of the mother tongue and culture of the country of origin'. The first draft of this directive applied to the education of children of nationals of EEC member states *and* of non-member states but the revised draft eliminates the latter requirement, partly in respnse to British pressure. However, the Department of Education and Science has stated in 1977 that no distinction would be made in Britain between EEC and other immigrants, although it added that provision would depend upon the availability of resources. Given that patois is not officially defined as the dominant language in the British Caribbean, it is clearly not formally included within the provisions of this directive. The directive is therefore likely to be interpreted to have much more relevance to the education of Asian children. Very few mother tongue teaching classes have been provided in schools and most existing provisions are run after school or on Saturday by volunteers. Arguments in support of mother tongue teaching are usually based on social, psychological, educational and linguistic grounds and proposed provisions vary from teaching of the mother tongue to teaching in English and in the mother tongue. In February 1978, the ILEA Further and Higher Education sub-committee approved grant aid to a number of schemes teaching mother tongue languages to children outside normal school hours. The University of London Institute of Education is currently drawing a language map of Britain, identifying the types of provision that exist for the teaching of these languages and is studying the factors affecting patterns of bilingualism and language use. This project is funded until 1982.

Racism and the curriculum

The appearance of black children in British schools has served to expose the ethnocentric and racist bias in the curriculum and in textbooks.[6] Black children are usually taught about the history and culture of a white society by a white teacher, while the society and culture from which the child and his/her parents originate receives litle attention and is implicitly devalued, if not explicitly defined as 'inferior' or 'backward'. Textbooks used in the arts, humanities and social studies are commonly written in terms which favourably picture British (and European) history and legitimise the British Empire, and in so doing, advance common racist stereotypes of black people. Such a curriculum and such books have a dual effect, serving to encourage the expression of or reinforce racist ideas amongst white children and to lead to a negative self-concept and lower the self-esteem of black children.[7] It is for this reason that curriculum change is a matter which affects not only black children but all children. Accordingly, to introduce a 'Black Studies' course exclusively for black children without corresponding changes to the curriculum as a whole is at best only half a solution.

However, the available evidence suggests that the situation may be somewhat more complex. Milner's study in the early 1970s found that black children showed a strong preference for the dominant white group and a tendency to devalue their own group. However, a more recent study by Louden found no significant differences in self-esteem between West Indian, Asian and English adolescents.[8] In support of his data, he argued that there is no necessary, direct relationship between the racist elements in the dominant culture and black adolescents because the cultural environment is selectively filtered by black adolescents. Where they spend much of their time in a neighbourhood and school in the company of other black children, racist images and beliefs expressed in the wider society (and, in particular, within the education system) may be mediated or even negated. These different findings may be a function of a different time and context, or may reflect the existence of different dimensions of identity (self-concept and self-esteem) which do not vary simply with one another.[9] Nevertheless, Louden's findings do not allow one to conclude that there is, after all, no reason to consider curriculum change. This is because firstly, the existing curriculum affects white and black children, and secondly, the continued expression of racist images and ideas in the curriculum and textbooks can legitimately become the objects of discontent and agitation on the part of black children who have come to assert their blackness positively.

The response to these issues seems to be very varied. A study of the education of West Indians in London schools identified a wide range of activities which fall under the heading of multi-cultural or multi-ethnic education.[10] Some schools did include material about the cultures of societies other than Britain, although this was done in some cases without any emphasis upon the relationship between this information and the presence in Britain of people who themselves or whose parents came from these societies. In other schools, information about the culture and societies of the Caribbean and Indian sub-continent was taught to improve relations between black and white children. The survey also identified a number of schools where Black Studies was taught with the intention of developing a positive self-identity amongst black children; in some cases such courses were made available to all children on the grounds that white children should also appreciate the positive contribution and history of black people. But not all schools had made changes to their curriculum. Some defended their 'inactivity' on the grounds that these sorts of changes would highlight differences amongst children which did not previously exist or about which there was little awareness. Giles's study suggests that the attitude of the staff, and particularly that of the headmaster, is a crucial factor in bringing about curriculum change.

There have been demands for more organised and centralised action. The National Union of Teachers proposed to the Schools Council that all schoolchildren be taught the art, religion and history of the different ethnic minorities in Britain as part of a national school curriculum. This has not been implemented but a proposal to examine the school curriculum has begun at Goldsmiths College, London. The project, 'Studies in the Multi-Ethnic Curriculum', began in October 1978. To deal with racism in school textbooks the National Union of Teachers is in the process of drawing up a set of guidelines to aid teachers when selecting material suitable for multi-ethnic education.

Teachers and teachers' attitudes

Most teachers are white. There are no official statistics on the number of black teachers but available evidence suggests that it is very small. The Caribbean Teachers' Association estimated that only 0.15% of all teachers were of Caribbean origin. A study of 102 black teachers in London in the mid 1970s by the Society for Immigrant Teachers reported evidence of discrimination against black teachers: they found that the black teachers who were able to find jobs were employed mainly in 'ghetto areas' and were kept on the lowest pay scales.

Many educationalists now believe teacher expectations can seriously affect the actual performance of their pupils – a case of the self-fulfilling prophecy. One study has reported that although teachers have a fairly positive attitude to the Asian child, they tend to regard the West Indian child as a problem, especially in terms of classroom behaviour.[11] No doubt compounding the problem is Edwards's claim, previously mentioned, that teachers often have low expectations of achievement by West Indian pupils who use patois. There is also some evidence available which indicates on the one hand that explicit racist stereotypes are held by teachers, although this evidence is anecdotal,[12] and on the other, that teachers incorrectly believe that their white pupils do not hold racist beliefs and so make no explicit effort to challenge them, preferring not to raise the issue at all.[13]

One response to teachers' ignorance about the origins and cultures of black children, their racism and their tendency to stereotype and formulate low expectations of certain groups of black children is now, belatedly, thought to be through training, both prior to teaching and in-service. During the 1960s little attention was paid to the training implications of teaching in a multi-ethnic society. In 1973 the Select Committee on Race Relations and Immigration recommended that 'All students at colleges of education should be made aware that, whatever they teach, they will be doing so in a multi-cultural society.'[14] In 1974 the Community Relations Commission produced a report *Teacher Education for a Multi-Cultural Society* which examined the provisions for students, training and courses. It recommended that all students be given an awareness of the multi-cultural society through their courses. However, local authorities and colleges of education have been slow to respond and only a small number pay serious attention to the implications for training of teaching in a multi-ethnic society. A survey by the Community Relations Commission in 1977 confirmed that teacher training had not prepared staff for the needs of black pupils.[15]

The University of London Institute of Education runs a full-time one-year in-service course, leading to a Diploma, at Southlands College which is designed for qualified teachers with a minimum of five years' teaching experience, tutors concerned with the education of teachers for multi-cultural schools and young people in further education, local authority advisers and other educationalists. The course aims to develop and deepen understanding of the implications of education in a multi-cultural society.

An evaluation of in-service teacher training and multi-ethnic education funded by the DES is currently underway at Keele University. The aim of the study is to assess the effectiveness of such courses and provide evidence of their specific objectives, recruitment, distribution, content, methodology and above all, their consequences in the communities, schools and classrooms.

In order to try to increase the number of black teachers, some special courses have been established. In July 1977 the Secretary of State for Education and Science in the Green Paper *Education in Schools* (Cmnd 6869) drew attention to the special needs of people (in particular black people) with experience but who lack qualifications for teaching. In August 1978, the DES asked seven local education authorities to develop special courses to prepare such students for entry to higher education. The need for such courses has been primarily identified in the sphere of teacher training although the aim is to prepare students for entry into higher education generally. The courses started in autumn 1979 and are to be of at least one year's duration.

The Polytechnic of North London mounted an educational programme in 1978 designed to enable more black people to enter teaching training courses. The first year of the course provides an alternative means of entry to a B.Ed. course more suited to the needs of this particular group. The standard aimed at on completion of the course will be such as to enable students to undertake the B.Ed. with the same degree of success as students entering by other means.

Underachievement?

So far, the issues of language, curriculum and teachers' attitudes have been discussed largely in isolation from each other and from wider social factors including racial discrimination in other areas of social life. The issue that forces us to consider all these factors together is that of 'underachievement' or the 'low performance' of black children in British schools. However, the fact that under-achievement has been discussed primarily with reference to West Indian children should warn us not to jump too quickly to simplistic conclusions about the effects of racial discrimination and racism both within and outside the education if it is the case that Asian children are not 'underachieving'. This is not to deny that racism and discrimination are widespread, nor that they affect the educational achievement of black children, but to suggest that in analysing underachievement we are dealing with a wide range of additional factors, some of which, potentially, can offset the influence of racism and discrimination. The significance of this point is further emphasised by recent evidence, which we shall shortly see, which questions the very fact of underachievement amongst West Indian children.

What, then, is the evidence for underachievement? A literacy survey carried out by the ILEA on a small sample of inner London schools between 1968 and 1975 showed a wide gap in reading ability between West Indian and other children, and that the gap in performance increased as the children grew older.[16] Further and more recent evidence of underachievement by West Indian children compared with both white British and Asian children was presented in a 1978 report by Redbridge Community Relations Council.[17] The suggestion that it is West Indian and not Asian children who are underachieving is given support by the work of Taylor.[18] The Select Committee on Race Relations and Immigration concluded that the evidence made available to it clearly indicated relative under-achievement of West Indian children and called for a special inquiry into the causes.[19] The government reacted positively to this recom-mendation and announced in mid 1978 that an inquiry into the achievement and needs of black children in the education system and into preparing all children for involvement in a multi-ethnic society; within this general framework, special attention would be given to factors which affected the achievement of West Indian children.

However, not all research findings lead to the same conclusion. Driver's study of West Indian children aged between 12 and 16 years shows that they did better academically than their English classmates. Moreover, his research shows that West Indian girls are higher achievers than West Indian boys.[20] These findings are a further reminder that care must be taken about the extent to which one can generalise about the success and failure of all black children. This research has already been the subject of much criticism. Driver's findings could, of course, reflect a change over time, but they might also be a result of different methods of assessing performance and/or to the fact that some measures of achievement are culture-bound and biased against the black child.

However this apparent contradiction is resolved, there is evidence other than that of reading ability, school placement and examination results on which to draw to show that West Indian children are disadvantaged within the British education system. This evidence concerns the numbers and proportion of West Indian children assigned to schools for the educationally sub-normal (ESN). In 1972, the last year for which there are official statistics, West Indian children constituted 1.1% of all children in state schools and 4.9% of all children in ESN schools.[21] This overrepresentation has been the cause of much concern and dispute within the West Indian population since 1965, a concern which was loudly expressed to the Select Committee on Race Relations and Immigration in 1976–7 and which was echoed in the Committee's report. Coard has argued that this overrepresentation is a consequence of the cultural bias of tests used in the education system, to low teacher expectations and to poor self-esteem and self-concept.[22] Other research shows that teachers do tend to believe that West Indian children have language and learning problems as well as behavioural and family problems.[23] Significantly, yet other research has shown that at least some Head Teachers are of the opinion that a significant number of West Indian children in ESN schools should not, in fact, be there.[24]

The explanation for educational underachievement and overrepresentation in ESN schools must extend beyond the operation of the education system, important though that is. There is now abundant evidence available which shows that the material and emotional circumstances of home life, which are in turn determined by level of income *inter alia*, have a substantial effect upon the educational achievement of all children.[25] Insofar as the parents of black children are disadvantaged in terms of the jobs that they do and the quality of housing that they occupy, one would expect their children to be disadvantaged within the educational system for these reasons too. This material disadvantage is compounded by the effect of racism and racial discrimination. So, for example, the material disadvantages which are shared with the rest of the working class can be especially significant for West Indian families, as is evidenced in the case of nursery provision.

Nursery provision

Responsibility for the under-fives is currently divided between the DES and the DHSS, the former having responsibility for nursery education and the latter for day-care. The shortage of provision for the under-fives is a problem which concerns most parents but which mainly affects those living in the most deprived areas. It is an issue of particular importance to working mothers and to single parents who are most likely to be in need of day care or nursery facilities for their young children. Furthermore a child's academic achievement and general development is thought by many educationalists to have its roots in the child's experience before the age of five. Evidence indicates that black mothers are more likely than white mothers to be working (see Chapter 3), that there is a disproportionate number of single parent families among West Indians, and a disproportionate number of black children in care (see Chapter 3). Since day care tends to be regarded as a preventive social service, priority being given to children who would otherwise be in need of full-time residential care, many mothers are forced to turn to illegal child minders where facilities are often overcrowded and inadequate.[26]

Government responses

The response of government to the presence of black children in British schools has been *ad hoc* and at times contradictory. The first 'official' educational advice appeared in 1963 in a Ministry of Education pamphlet.[27] This pointed out the need for a carefully planned intensive course of teaching of English as a second language at primary and secondary school level. The pamphlet also gave general advice on educational arrangements for immigrant pupils. At this time, however, there were virtually no trained teachers in English as a second language, nor were there teaching materials. Until the publication of this pamphlet advice was given by HM Inspectors to local education authorities and schools. This was followed in 1965 by circular 1/65 in which local authorities with a substantial number of immigrant pupils were invited to apply for increases in their teacher quota. However, no additional financial assistance was made available.

In 1964 the Commonwealth Immigrants Advisory Council, set up in 1963 by the then Conservative Government to advise the Home Secretary on matters concerning the welfare and 'integration' of immigrants, published its second report.[28] In this it claimed, among other things, that one of the disadvantages of concentrations of immigrant pupils was that they retarded the progress of indigenous pupils by interruption of the normal school routine and concluded that as a last resort dispersal would be necessary. The drafting of this report coincided with a protest in Southall in 1963 organised by white parents who were threatening to withdraw their children from two primary schools because they were concerned that concentrations of black pupils would adversely affect the educational progress of their own children.

In June 1965 circular 7/65 was issued which recommended that the proportion of immigrant pupils in any one school should not exceed 30% of the total. The Government stated: 'As the proportion of immigrant children in a school or class increases the problems will become more difficult to solve, and the chances of assimilation more remote.' The DES also stated that the only grounds for dispersal were educational need although the practice suggested otherwise as it was mainly black children who were 'dispersed'. In August 1965 the official dispersal policy was set out in the White Paper *Immigration from the Commonwealth*. The White Paper basically reiterated circular 7/65 but was presented as a multi-purpose policy, as an aid to integrating immigrant children, as a way to prevent a fall in school standards and as a help to the organisation of special English classes.

E. J. B. Rose et al. have pointed to a basic contradiction between the earlier pamphlet *English for Immigrants*, circular 1/65 and circular 7/65 and the White Paper *Immigration from the Commonwealth*.[29] The first two in fact called for the bringing together of immigrant children for English classes in one school, the second suggested that the teaching of English was a goal but 'such arrangements can more easily be made, and the integration of the immigrants more easily achieved, if the proportion of the immigrant children in a school is not allowed to rise too high'. This contradiction is significant because it suggests that the issue of concentration rather than language need predominated. As Julia McNeal said 'the bogey has not been discrimination – less favourable treatment – but concentration. This has been condemned not so much because it might lead to less favourable treatment, but often because it was seen as the development of foreign enclaves within British culture and society'.[30]

The Department of Education and Science emphasised dispersal but it was left to the local authorities to interpret the recommendations. Six local authorities implemented dispersal by 'busing' black children to other schools (Ealing, Bradford, West Bromwich, Halifax, Huddersfield and Hounslow); others, such as ILEA and Birmingham, rejected it: and others found it practically impossible to keep to the suggested limit of 30% and abandoned the idea. There was also disagreement over the principle as to whether or not children should be moved on grounds of origin as opposed to educational need. In May 1978 Ealing, one of the last remaining authorities to operate the policy, finally agreed to abandon it after an inquiry initiated against the authority by the Race Relations Board in 1972. Bradford is the only authority to date which still operates a policy of dispersal. The implications of the dispersal policy was that black pupils arrested the educational progress of white pupils. However research carried out by the Inner London Education Authority on the performance of black and white school children aged 8–11 concluded that there was no evidence to justify dispersal.[31]

Up to this point the recommended government policies had no statistical base but in 1966 the DES began to collect statistics on immigrant children, although that was discontinued in 1972 as already indicated.

Coincidental with this, in the early 1970s the DES were still focusing their attention on the 'immigrant' pupil (when an increasing proportion of black pupils were British-born) and published three surveys. The first was concerned with an assessment of attainment and intelligence of immigrant pupils.[32] The second was concerned with general policies and practices in the education of immigrant children and indicated a modification in the views of the DES on dispersal.[33] The third was concerned with the need for continued special help for immigrant pupils after the initial stage of English teaching at the secondary school stage. The survey concluded that the majority of schools in the areas concerned could 'undertake much more positive thinking and constructive action in matters relating to the linguistic, intellectual and social needs of second-phase immigrant pupils'.[34]

More recent government initiatives have been discussed in Chapter 2. These include the establishment of Educational Priority

Areas and of the Educational Disadvantage Unit which itself set up the Centre for Information and Advice on Educational Disadvantage. All three of these initiatives were concerned with the overall pattern of educational disadvantage, although it was also thought that black children would benefit as a matter of course.

In addition, within the DES and local authorities, there are a number of special units and appointments which have been created to deal with the needs of black pupils. The DES have established a Multi-Ethnic Inspectorate which is concerned with all aspects of multi-ethnic education and the Inner London Education Authority have established a similar body with similar functions. In other areas, local education authorities have appointed staff with responsibility for multi-ethnic education. The functions and job titles of these appointments vary considerably and the Runnymede Trust is currently examining their role and function.

Outside of government machinery, independent organisations and pressure groups have been set up, such as the National Association for Multi-Racial Education (NAME). NAME was established in 1965 and was initially concerned with the needs of black pupils but has since broadened its perspectives to include the educational needs of all children in Britain. The organisation aims to campaign for changes in the educational system which will further the development of a just multi-ethnic society.

Notes
1. H. E. R. Townsend and E. Brittan, *Organisation in Multi-Racial Schools* (London: National Federation for Education and Research, 1972).
2. H. E. R. Townsend, *Immigrant Pupils in England: The LEA Response* (London: National Federation for Education and Research, 1971).
3. National Union of Teachers, *Section 11: A National Union of Teachers Report* (London: NUT, 1978).
4. E. J. B. Rose et al., *Colour and Citizenship* (London; Oxford University Press, 1969).
5. V. Edwards, *The West Indian Language Issue in British Schools* (London: Routledge and Kegan Paul, 1979); R. Miles, *Between Two Cultures? The Case of Rastafarianism,* SSRC Research Unit on Ethnic Relations Library Paper no. 10, 1978.
6. S. Hatch, *Coloured People in School Textbooks, Race* 1962, Vol. 4, no. i, pp. 63–72; S. G. Zimet, *Print and Prejudice* (London: Hodder and Stoughton, 1976).
7. D. Milner, *Children and Race* (Harmondsworth: Penguin, 1975).
8. D. Loudon, 'Self-esteem and locus of control: some findings on immigrant adolescents in Britain', *New Community*, 1978, Vol. 6, no. 3, pp. 218–34. Also 'Self-esteem and locus of control in minority group adolescents', *Ethnic and Racial Studies*, 1970, Vol. 1, pp. 196–217.
9. See for example, L. Young and C. Bagley 'Identity, self-esteem and evaluation of colour and ethnicity in young children in Jamaica and London', *New Community*, 1979, Vol. 7, no. 2, pp. 154–69.
10. R. Giles, *The West Indian Experience in British Schools* (London: Heinemann, 1977).

11. Townsend and Brittan, op. cit. See also G. Davis, *Classroom Stress and School Achievement* in V. S. Khan (ed.), *Minority Families in Britain* (London: Macmillan, 1979).

12. Milner, op. cit.

13. 'Race and teachers: the Schools Council Study', *New Society*, Vol 16, 1980, pp. 366–8. See also W. Yult et al., 'Children of West Indian immigrants, II, Intellectual performance and reading attainment', *Journal of Child Psychology and Psychiatry*, 1975, 16.

14. Select Committee on Race Relations and Immigration, session 1972–73, *Education*, Vol. 1, p. 56, para. 9.

15. Community Relations Commission, *Urban Deprivation, Racial Inequality and Social Policy: A Report*, London, 1977.

16. A. N. Little, *Educational Policies for Multi-Racial Areas*. Goldsmith College Inaugural Lecture, 1978.

17. Redbridge Community Relations Council and Black Peoples Progressive Association *Cause for Concern:* West Indian Pupils in Redbridge, Redbridge CRC, 1978.

18. J. H. Taylor, 'Newcastle upon Tyne: Asian pupils do better than whites', *British Journal of Sociology*, 1973, Vol. 54, no. 4.

19. Select Committee on Race Relations and Immigration, *The West Indian Community* (London: HMSO, 1977).

20. G. Driver, 'Cultural competence, social power and school achievement: West Indian pupils in the West Midlands', *New Community*, 1977, Vol. 5, no. 4, pp. 353–9. Also 'How West Indians do better at school (especially the girls)', *New Society*, 17 January 1980, pp. 111–14.

21. S. Tomkinson, 'West Indian children and ESN schooling', *New Community*, 1978, Vol. 6, no. 2, pp. 235–42.

22. B. Coard, *How the West Indian Child is made Educationally Sub-normal in the British School System* (London: New Beacon Books, 1971).

23. E. Brittan 'Teacher-opinion on aspects of school life, pupils and teachers', *Educational Research*, 1976, Vol. 8, no. 3. Also Giles, op. cit. and Driver, 1979, op. cit.

24. Townsend and Brittan, op. cit.

25. See, for example, J. W. B. Douglas, *The Home and the School* (London: Panther, 1964); J. Raynor and J. Harden (eds.), *Equality and City Schools* (London: Routledge and Kegan Paul, 1973).

26. M. Pollak, *Today's Three-year-olds in London* (London: Heinemann, 1972).

27. Ministry of Education, *English for Immigrants*, Pamphlet no. 43 (London: HMSO, 1963).

28. Commonwealth Immigrants Advisory Council, *Second Report* (Cmnd 2266), London, HMSO, 1964.

29. E. J. B. Rose et al., op. cit.

30. J. McNeal, 'Education' in S. Abbott (ed.), *The Prevention of Racial Discrimination in Britain* (London: Oxford University Press, 1971).

31. Little, op. cit.

32. Department of Education and Science, *Potential and Progress in a Second Culture: Education Survey no. 10* (London: HMSO, 1971).

33. Department of Education and Science, *The Education of Immigrants: Education Survey no. 13* (London: HMSO, 1971).

34. Department of Education and Science, *The Continuing Needs of Immigrants: Education Survey no. 14* (London: HMSO, 1972), p. 27.

6 Health and Social Services

In Chapter 6 the questions of whether black people in Britain have any 'special needs' with respect to the provision and operation of the health and social services and, if so, what responses have been forthcoming from the various bodies concerned are considered. This raises the following more general issues which, in order to avoid confusion, must be stated at the outset.

First, there is the question of interpreting the meaning and implications of the notion of 'special needs'. If any group can be shown to exhibit a higher incidence of certain illnesses, or to utilise a particular social service more often, than another group, it may be argued that that group is thereby a special 'burden' on the welfare state. As an example of this argument, one may cite the political 'scandal' created by prominent Conservative politicians in the 1960s about the utilisation of hospital beds by black mothers. In response to this sort of argument, it must be emphasised that black people from the New Commonwealth, by virtue of their unqualified right to settle and work in Britain (at least up until 1962), had the right to use immediately and fully facilities of the welfare state that were made available according to need and without reference to any specific contribution. Moreover, one cannot conclude from evidence that shows, for example, that black women use more maternity hospital beds than white women that black people therefore make greater use or place excessive demand upon the National Health Service. Such a conclusion can only be drawn if evidence is available which compares use and non-use of *all* NHS facilities. For instance, greater use of NHS maternity beds may be 'offset' by lower use of geriatric beds. In sum, one must distinguish between 'special needs' which are particular and specific and overall demand or use which is general.

Second, use of health and social services by black people is primarily a consequence of their socioeconomic circumstances and certainly not because they are physically different from the majority of the population. However, it is also the case that the distinct cultures of the different ethnic groups that comprise the British black population can lead to social situations or behaviour which comes to require the intervention of social service departments. For example, in the Caribbean, there is much less disapproval of children being born outside of marriage and it is common for women to raise children without the material and emotional support of the father but with the assistance instead of the woman's mother. In Britain, with the grandmother more likely to be absent, unmarried mothers may come to use the resources of the social services.

Third, cultural differences are a crucial factor in assessing the nature of the service provided. The cultural assumptions which underlie the provision of services are often only made apparent when a member of a group with a different culture comes to use that service. For example, the meat-based diet of the British population is made evident when a vegetarian Hindu enters a hospital for treatment. The greater importance attached to family organisation and family honour by Pakistanis in comparison with white British is made evident when a social worker attempts to intervene in a situation when a boy runs away from home in an attempt to avoid an arranged marriage.

Finally, analysis of the use of health and social services by black people should be made in the context of the nature and operation of the welfare state as a whole. This is important because the extent to which the needs of black people are or are not recognised and/or met have to be considered in relation to the effectiveness of the services in meeting the needs of all users of these services. Space prevents us from expanding and illustrating this point.

Health

There is no systematic or detailed evidence available about the health of black people in Britain. It is therefore difficult to draw any clear conclusions about different patterns of illness amongst black people in comparison with the white population and, consequently, the extent to which any such differences are recognised and being catered for. The evidence that does exist is scattered and piecemeal and so the information and discussion here must be regarded as tentative. Some of it does suggest different patterns of health and illness between black and white people, but it also shows different patterns between different groups within the black population. However, following on from a point made at the start of this chapter, few of these studies attempted to discover whether the white population was more prone than the black population to certain illnesses. One must not therefore confuse the issue of special need with that of overall demand.

In 1967 the National Institute of Economic and Social Research (NIESR) published the findings of an investigation into the net economic effect of demands made by (black) immigrants upon the health and welfare services.[1] It identified three factors which were then supposed to reflect the most significant differences in demands. These were the higher proportion of immigrant hospital births, the higher incidence of tuberculosis amongst immigrants and the higher (but falling) incidence of venereal disease. There appears to be little evidence that any of these factors indicates continuing and serious special needs. There has been a general movement away from home confinement and the number of cases of pulmonary tuberculosis notified in Great Britain has declined from 28,141 in 1959 to 11,400 in 1969 and a provisional 8,959 in 1976.[2] There is little recent information on the incidence of venereal disease amongst black people.

More recently in its evidence to the Royal Commission on the National Health Service in 1977 the Community Relations Commission presented information which showed that certain sections of the black population do have potential or actual special demands on the NHS.[3] The first concerned low birth weight which is defined as 2.5 kg or less and is regarded as a major associate of infant mortality, morbidity and aberrant development. Available information suggests that Asian babies in Britain have low birth weights and high levels of perinatal and infant mortality in comparison with the indigenous population. In 1971 Bamford found that between 1967 and 1969, 15.1% of 3024 babies born to Asian women in Bradford were of low birth weight, compared with 8.6% of 12,694 babies born to indigenous women.[4] The Community Relations Commission drew attention to the inadequate investigation into the reasons for weight differentials and expressed concern at the low take-up of ante-natal and post-natal care services.

The Community Relations Commission, in its evidence to the Royal Commission on the National Health Service, identified certain dietary deficiencies amongst Asians: 'Anaemia caused by iron deficiency or Vitamin B12 deficiency is almost certainly more common among Asians, particularly among vegetarian Hindus,

whose diet is devoid of easily assimilated iron from animal sources.'
Roberts et al. measured haemoglobin, serum vitamin B12 (ref 3)
and serum of red cell folate levels in 322 pregnant immigrant women
at their first ante-natal booking; 126 women were followed up at 34
weeks gestation and post-natally. The Indian, East African Indian,
Pakistani and Bangladeshi women showed significantly lower serum
vitamin B12 levels than European women. Serum vitamin B12 levels
were lower among Hindus and Sikhs than Moslems. The West
Indian, Indian and East African Indian women also showed significantly lower initial haemoglobin levels than immigrants from
Europe.[5]

In addition to 'normal' anaemia, two specific anaemic conditions
are known to affect certain groups of black people. Sickle cell
anaemia, an inherited difficulty in the manufacture of haemoglobin,
affects West Indian and African, and thalassemia, also an inherited
anaemia, affects Cypriot babies. These conditions are much rarer
among the indigenous white population and few facilities exist to
deal with the complaint.

Third, there is the question of the incidence of rickets and osteomalacia. Both rickets and its adult equivalent, osteomalacia, are
thought to be caused by vitamin D deficiency. Rickets has virtually
disappeared from the indigenous population, largely because of the
fortification of National Dried Milk during the Second World War
with vitamin D. However, it has reappeared to some extent amongst
the indigenous white population of Glasgow, and studies suggest
that it is also particularly prevalent among the Asian populations.
This is thought to be a result of a combination of a diet which is low
in fish, margarine and dairy products and a low exposure to sunlight,
particulary amongst Asian girls and women. Goel examined 200
Asian and 300 African, Chinese and Scottish children for clinical,
biochemical and radiological evidence of vitamin D deficiency.
Twenty-five of the Asian compared with seven in the non-Asian
group showed evidence of rickets.[6] Investigations among different
sub-groups of Ugandan Asians suggest that an enrichment of chapati
flour with vitamin D would benefit those groups of Asians whose
vulnerability is increased by their diet.[7] However, nothing has been
done so far to implement such a programme.

Turning from 'physical' to 'mental' health, the limited evidence is
again somewhat contradictory. It can be argued that migrating from
a poor agricultural village in Pakistan or Jamaica to a British
industrial city is a stressful experience in itself. This may be com-

pounded by the experience of racial discrimination and of a culture which is seen as threatening certain key values of the migrant. The consequence, it may be predicted, will be higher rates of psychiatric breakdown amongst the black, immigrant population. Some studies give support to this argument[8] whereas others report a low rate of mental illness among some groups of migrants.[9] Rack has suggested that this debate be put to one side, at least in the current state of knowledge. He argues that consideration be given instead to the much more specific questions about the access of particular ethnic groups to treatment facilities and about differences in the reporting of symptoms of illness by people from a culture which is quite different from that of the doctor.[10]

From his own casework experience, Rack argues that diagnosing mental illness is greatly dependent upon how the patient reports his/her symptoms and the pattern of symptoms as presented. He goes on to say that Asians are more likely to focus their attention upon physical complaints and to identify illness not in terms of internal distress but in terms of the extent to which the person is or remains capable of fulfilling his or her social duties. Rack also argues that diagnosis of paranoid states can be difficult when the patient comes from a society where belief in supernatural forces (e.g. the evil eye) is widespread. Ballard has summarised this point most clearly: 'in a situation where magico-religious beliefs are pervasive, the "rational" and the "magical", the physical and the mental, are not always so separable. Very often allegations about supernatural forces may be a means of making statements about real social relationships. However, in the absence of an understanding of the code, such communications may seem bizarre and deluded, evidence perhaps of schizophrenia.[11] In sum, insofar as there are cultural differences in how people experience and account for their mental and physical conditions, what counts as mental illness can be problematic. This will clearly affect the numbers of persons who voluntarily seek out treatment and requires the psychiatrist to be aware of the cultural background of all of his/her patients.

There does, then, appear to be some evidence that the black population, particularly the Asian population, does have special health needs. These concern diseases and conditions associated with dietary deficiencies and child health. However, the conclusion reached by the NIESR study also requires repetition: 'largely because of their age structure, immigrant families make smaller demands on the Health Services than other families; and this is likely to hold true for some time to come' (page 3).[12]

Social Services

As with health, information on the relationship between black people and the social services provision must be collected from many disparate studies. There has, however, been a more systematic compilation of the responses of local and national government to the perceived needs of black people. These needs – additional to those of the general population – were recognised and discussed by the Community Relations Commission's report on urban deprivation.[13] This report acknowledged the definition used by those who administer the social services – that these services are provided for those in need or disadvantaged in some way. Consequently, when social service departments operate in relation to groups of people, these are defined in terms of need; for example, the elderly, the handicapped, children in care, etc. They are unwilling to identify particular ethnic groups as requiring special attention or having special needs as such, but rather allocate individuals from such groups to a category of need. However, the Community Relations Commission was at pains to demonstrate that 'urban deprivation and social disadvantage experienced by ethnic minorities differ from those of other residents in urban deprived areas (page v)'. To support this claim, the Commission's report identified a number of areas of disadvantage facing black people in their relationship with the social services.

The first concerned the problem of communication. Language differences and proficiency have serious implications for the dissemination of information by social services and health departments, yet the language barrier has not been acknowledged constructively. The Political and Economic Planning (PEP) survey rated 42% of Asians in the sample as speaking English only slightly or not at all.[14] Furthermore, women are less likely to be fluent in English than men, and older women are unlikely ever to be sufficiently fluent. Some of the problems in communication faced by non-English speaking people are also shared by those people from the Caribbean who use a non-standard dialect of English.

There are two main areas in which improvements are needed. Black people need information about their welfare rights, the services provided and special issues of significance. A study of one-parent families in Haringey found that black families knew less about, and claimed fewer grants for unsupported and low income families than the rest of the population.[15] Translations of welfare rights etc. have been organised by several departments and an increasing amount of health education material is available in languages other than English. However, a great deal more could be done to disseminate information. The survey of Asians and the Health Service by Wandsworth Council for Community Relations found that only 13 out of 46 Area Health Authorities with high ethnic minority populations had employed interpreters, and only six of these authorities mentioned the use of language cards and phrase books, and these were predominantly used in hospitals.[16] However, language cards and phrase books are of value only to those literate in their own language. In addition, the rights and powers of social workers, for example the power to take children into care or commit people for mental health treatment, must be clearly explained to black people who are often unaware of the far reaching powers of social services departments.

Second, there is the question of children in care. There is considerable evidence that a disproportionate number of children in care are black. A survey in the London Borough of Wandsworth in 1973–4 found that 48% of all children received into care were of West Indian origin, and they tended to be younger than white children in care.[17] This is likely to be because black people are overrepresented in those groups whose characteristics presuppose their children to be received into care, e.g. single parents without support of kin, inferior housing conditions, etc. The high number of black children in care is coupled with a shortage of foster parents, and in particular black foster parents. However, the shortage of black foster parents is in part caused by the inflexibility of the social services departments whose strict requirements regarding accommodation etc. prevent a large number of black parents from qualifying for fostering. In an attempt to circumvent this problem, nine London boroughs ran an experimental fostering campaign in 1975–76 of black parents for black children. The campaign had an educative role in informing black people about the plight of black children in care and in helping to bridge the communication gap between black people and social work agencies.[18] But initiatives of this sort are unusual.

Third, there is some evidence that elderly black people face special problems. The black population is relatively young on average with few old people. According to the 1971 Census, 26,400 over-60-year-olds were born in the New Commonwealth and living in Britain. The number and proportion of elderly black people is gradually increasing with longer established settlement. A report produced by Age Concern in 1974 found that while elderly black people have needs similar to those of the general population, they have additional needs resulting from racial discrimination, differences in culture, insecurity in an alien environment, remoteness from friends and relatives and a sense of isolation.[19] These factors have implications for the services which local authorities provide, such as day centres, meals on wheels, old people's homes, etc. Special provisions are rarely made and separate provisions are even more unusual. A Community Relations Commission report found that a local authority had refused to support an Urban Aid application to provide for elderly Asians, even though the department was aware of their special needs, on the grounds that separate provisions were not compatible with their policy.[20] An Asian housing project has been established in Wandsworth through the Housing Corporation, but this is the first scheme of its type. Most provisions for elderly black people are, in fact, organised by the communities themselves but the problems of finance impose severe limitations.

Finally, consideration must be given to one-parent families. The incidence of one-parent families varies with ethnic group and is particularly characteristic of the West Indian population because, at least in part, of the recreation of West Indian family patterns in Britain. The *General Household Survey 1972* reported that 13% of West Indian households were comprised of families with a single parent, compared with 9% in the general population.[21] This, together with the extent of full-time female employment in minority groups, probably leads to a greater demand for pre-school day-care provision from the black population than from the general population. In its report on day-care for young children and opportunities for working parents, the Equal Opportunities Commission noted that more mothers work now than at any other period during peace-time, yet the local authority target figure for day-care places remains 8 per 1000 under-fives.[22] The priority waiting lists alone stood at 12,601 in 1976 and local authorities are under no obligation even to assess the total level of demand in their areas.

In sum, although the evidence is limited, it does suggest that certain groups of black people are disproportionately represented or pose new issues within the existing, traditional categories of need used by the social services. To what extent overrepresentation is matched by underrepresentation in other categories of need is not known. In order to explain this overrepresentation one must consider both the effect of racial discrimination (which tends to confine them to low-pay jobs and poor-quality housing) and the respective cultural distinctiveness of the different sections of the black population.

The latter point is important in a second sense, which can now be discussed. Ballard has argued that social service departments should make themselves aware of the culturally specific beliefs and behaviour of the different ethnic minorities in Britain, not only because such knowledge should bring about an understanding of behaviour which seems confusing, but also because social service departments might discover ethnically specific resources which can help deal with certain problems and needs.[23] He points to the importance of family and community structure to Indian and Pakistani migrants to Britain, arguing that intervention by social workers must take account of the importance placed on family honour and communal involvement if it is to be in any way successful. This raises the general issue of the response of social services to the presence of black people in Britain and in particular the question of social service training and the extent to which black people themselves are taking up positions in the various sectors of the social services.

The limited evidence suggests that the response of the social services to black clients has varied considerably. This is probably in part a result of the absence of clear guidelines from the Department of Health and Social Security on the provision of services in multi-ethnic areas. A joint investigation by the Commission for Racial Equality and the Association of Directors of Social Services (CRE/ADSS) found that the responses initiated in different areas were related more to individual judgements than to a systematic assessment of needs.[24] The report further found that those authorities that did respond did so in very different ways which could not be justified in terms of differences in need. One of the main areas of ambiguity and uncertainty has been over the question of collecting information on ethnic origin. It is a particularly sensitive topic which many local authorities seem reluctant to approach in the absence of clear central guidance. The CRE/ADSS survey of 62 social services departments found that only three kept records of the ethnic origin of their staff and only seven kept records of the ethnic origin of their clients.

The recruitment of black staff and the training of staff on the needs of ethnic minorities clearly has a bearing on communication problems and any under-utilisation of services as well as on the quality of the service provided. The CRE/ADSS report found 48 out of 62 departments had ethnic minority group staff in field or residential social work. In reply to a question on the extent to which departments had made special efforts to recruit black staff, 51 out of 62 said they were not making any special efforts. A distinction should be made between employing black staff for posts similar to any other staff and employing them for specific work within their own communities. Some authorities who have employed black staff have employed them to work primarily with ethnic minority communities. Many black employees do not want to work only with black clients, since the implication is that they are only useful in this capacity. If such a practice became general, it would effectively create a completely separate service for black people which could isolate both clients and staff. However, while black people are employed in social service departments they can serve as consultants, providing information and advice when it is required.

The presence of ethnic minorities has special implications for the skills and training of social workers. A proper understanding of the background, culture, special needs and problems of all clients is essential if an effective service is to be provided and black clients are certainly not an exception. While many individuals and departments recognise the need for special training and skills if black people are to receive an effective service, remarkably little has, in fact, been done to ensure this. Catherine Jones, in a study published in 1977, found that only nine out of 13 social services departments in areas with a black population offered some kind of special training for social workers working with black people.[25] She also found that the type of training varied considerably, and often consisted of little more than an occasional seminar. A similar finding was reported by the CRE/ADSS survey, which found that 22 out of 62 departments had no organised training of staff on the needs of black clients. A survey of 57 Area Health Authorities in selected regions, by Wandsworth Council for Community Relations found that only 14 authorities mentioned in-service training of staff.[26] Cross has reported that 50% of his sample of social workers claimed that their training did not equip them to deal with black people.[27]

The specific training that their working in the social services require is similar to that required by other professional groups, such as teachers. Some initiatives have been taken. A special project funded by the King Edward's Hospital Fund and the DHSS is planning to develop training materials, which will give nursing staff and other health workers additional information on the background of Asian patients. The DHSS is also funding Goldsmiths College to produce a training pack for in-service training for social workers. The Association for Multi-racial Social Work, established in 1978, aims to encourage the employment and training of members of ethnic minorities in social work and to press for the introduction of training to prepare all social workers to be able to practise in a multi-racial society.

This limited and uneven response reflects both financial constraints and the orientation and beliefs of decision-makers in social service departments. Cross reports that decision-makers in his survey referred to a lack of money as a key factor in making decisions about responding to black clients. He found that little use had been made of Urban Aid because of administrative complications and the financial restrictions of the scheme itself. The CRE/ADSS survey found that only 16 out of 62 social service departments had made any use of Section 11 of the *Local Government Act 1966* as a potential source of finance and that the Department of Health and Social Security had done little to draw the attention of local authorities to the possible use of this source. Cross also reports that there was concern that socal service departments should not be seen to discriminate in favour of any particular group, a value position that is consistent with the view that clients are to be defined in terms of their common disadvantage. Decision-makers interviewed by Cross additionally reported that they had difficulty in finding well-trained staff who would operate in 'inner city' areas, but few said that they had made any special effort to recruit black staff or staff who had special knowledge of working with black people.

In the light of all this evidence, there is no reason not to agree with the conclusion of the CRE/ADSS report that 'the response of social service departments to the existence of multi-racial communities has been patchy, piecemeal and lacking in strategy'.[28]

Notes

1. K. Jones, *Immigrants and the Social Services* (London: National Institute Economic Review, 1967).
2. Department of Health and Social Security, *Health and Social Services*, London, 1977.
3. Community Relations Commission, *Evidence to the Royal Commission on the National Health Service* (London: Community Relations Commission, 1977).
4. F. N. Bamford, 'Immigrant Mother and her Child', *British Medical Journal*, 1971, no. 1, pp. 276–80.
5. P. D. Roberts, et al., 'Vitamin B12 Status in Pregnancy among Immigrants to Britain', *British Medical Journal*, 1973, no. 3, pp. 67–72.
6. K. M. Goel, et al., 'Forid and Sub-clinical Rickets among Immigrant Children in Glasgow', *The Lancet*, 1967, no. 1, pp. 1141–5.

7. S. P. Hunt, et al., 'Vitamin D Status in Different Sub-groups of British Asians', *British Medical Journal*, 1976, no. 6, pp. 1351–4.
8. L. K. Hensi, 'Psychiatric Mobility of West Indian Immigrants', *Social Psychiatry*, 1967, no. 2; F. Mashmi, 'Community Psychiatric Problems among Birmingham Immigrants', *Journal of Social Psychiatry*, 1968, no. 2.
9. R. Cochrane, 'Immigration and Mental Hospital Admissions: A Study of Rates for England and Wales 1971', *Social Psychiatry*, 1976, no. 11.
10. P. Rack, 'Diagnosing Mental Illness: Asians and the Psychiatric Services' in V. S. Khan (ed.), *Minority Families in Britain* (London: MacMillan, 1979).
11. R. Ballard, 'Ethnic Minorities and the Social Services' in V. S. Khan, op. cit.
12. Jones, op. cit.
13. Community Relations Commission, *Urban Deprivation, Racial Inequality and Social Policy* (London: Community Relations Commission, 1977). See also C. Cross, *Ethnic Minorities in the Inner City* (London: Commission for Racial Equality, 1978).
14. D. Smith, *The Facts of Racial Disadvantage* (London: Political and Economic Planning, 1976).
15. *Families and their Needs*, Vol. 1, Haringey Hunt.
16. Wandsworth Council for Community Relations, *Asians and the Health Service*, 1978.
17. London Borough of Wandsworth, *Statistics of the Social Service Department*, 1974.
18. Association of British.Adoption and Fostering Agencies, *The Soul Kids Campaign*, 1977.
19. Age Concrn, *Elderly Ethnic Minorities*, 1974.
20. Community Relations Commission, 1977, op. cit.
21. OPCS, *General Household Survey* (London: HMSO, 1972).
22. Equal Opportunities Commission, *'I Want to Work but What About the Kids. . . .'*, 1978.
23. Ballard, op. cit.
24. Association of Directors of Social Services and Commission for Racial Equality, *Multi-Racial Britain: The Social Services Response*, London, 1978.
25. C. Jones, *Immigration and Social Policy in Britain* (London: Tavistock, 1977).
26. Wandsworth Council for Community Relations, op. cit.
27. Cross, op. cit.
28. Op. cit., page 14.

7 The Politics of Statistics

Throughout this book statistics from a wide variety of sources have been used and commented on. There has been particular emphasis on official statistics, i.e. those produced by government departments. These sources have been developed in a largely piecemeal way and some sources are more detailed and comprehensive than others. In some areas there is very little data collection at all. It is pertinent to ask why statistics of this kind are collected and to what use they might be put. Why is the black population of interest? Monitoring of immigration might be justified on the grounds that there is a need to monitor the numbers entering the country who are born overseas, since they may have special needs in the areas of language and health. But what is the interest in the black population *born* in Britain? Would there be such an interest in this if we lived in a literally colour blind society?

Collection of statistics on immigrants has been carried on for some time although the political and public interest has focused primarily on statistics about black immigrants from the New Commonwealth. Little public or political attention is paid to statistics relating to white immigrants or to the number of immigrants entering Britain with work permits since 1971. The new emphasis is upon the collection of statistics about black immigrants and their British-born children and this has served to re-emphasise pre-existing terminological confusion. As the immigrant population from the Caribbean and the Indian sub-continent have remained separately endogamous, their children tend to share their parents' physical characteristics. Hence, one is able to refer to a British-born black population. However, it is not just physical characteristics which are treated as a sign of difference and thereby attributed with social significance, but also their various cultural characteristics. This has led to the idea that what is of statistical interest is 'ethnic origin'. This notion is misleading because the statistical (and political) interest is, in fact, a population which is identified by both physical and cultural characteristics. Moreover, as the term 'ethnic' is used to refer to a group which maintains its own cultural distinctiveness, it is inaccurate to refer to Indians and Pakistanis as 'ethnic groups' because culture and self-identification is primarily centred on village and region of origin. Hence we have placed the notion of 'ethnic origin' in quotes to signal these ambiguities.

The last review of government statistics on immigration was by Claus Moser, then Director of the Central Statistical Office:

> Figures about migration into and out of the United Kingdom are more than just another component for making estimates of national population. They have an intrinsic interest and importance of their own, and in recent years interest in migration statistics in this country has been stimulated by some specific issues, and especially by the influx of New Commonwealth immigrants which began to occur in significant numbers in the late 1950s. This topic receives special emphasis in the latter sections of this article.
>
> Public policy and public discussion need to be informed by relevant and reliable data on such issues.
>
> The strong current interest in these matters gives a special importance to this and places on the Government Statistical Service a responsibility for disseminating information on sources and methods so that the available official statistics may be correctly interpreted and their limitations clearly understood.[1]

Moser is clearly arguing that statistics are needed for public policy decisions and public discussion about immigration. Although it appears that it is immigrants which are primarily of interest, the rest of the article confirms that it is the black population and not just immigrants which are actually being discussed.

Whilst the provision of accurate information for, say, classroom or bar-room debate is clearly important, it is the policy implications which are even more important. It is argued that accurate information is needed about the population in order to make rational and informed decisions in planning future policies. The statistics provide evidence of both the disadvantage and discrimination suffered by the black population. The implication is that this evidence will lead to policies to combat these problems. Until recently the collection of statistics on the basis of 'ethnic origin' was widely deplored as being discriminatory in itself, but now there is growing support for more statistics. The Commission for Racial Equality, for example, strongly supports the idea of 'ethnic' record-keeping.

Whilst there may be a large volume of support for 'ethnic' record-keeping, there is also growing opposition to the idea. Opposition is based on the grounds that it is racist and discriminatory to attempt to classify people according to their skin colour and 'ethnic origin'. The use of physical and cultural characteristics to identify different groups is a social process and, in the case of physical differentiation, cannot be justified by references to biological or genetic science. It is argued that the collection of such statistics only reinforces these socially created divisions. In a question which was proposed for the 1981 Census on 'ethnic origin', a black youth born in Britain, whose parents are from the West Indies, is classified as 'West Indian', though he may never have seen those islands, whereas a white youth whose parents were born in Australia is identified simply as white, or white (European descent). In this instance, it is argued the black person is singled out. There is also the argument against record-keeping that the volume of information on the individual already collected by government is excessive and, with modern computer technology, there is a growing danger of misuse of this information. Government departments, local authorities and the police between them already hold enough information to compile a comprehensive profile of every UK resident. Central government has declared that it has no intention of linking those data banks now held separately, but there is no guarantee that this will not happen in the future. Patricia Hewitt has described how, in 1971, William Whitelaw, MP gave a public undertaking that 'information about individual people or families will under no circumstances be released to any authority outside the census organisation itself' (Hansard, 20 April 1971). Despite this promise, OPCS undertook, on behalf of the DHSS, a follow-up survey of ex-nurses, whose names and addresses were obtained from the individual census returns.[2]

Another reason for opposition is the disquiet felt about the political uses to which information may be put. Given the strength of political expression of racism in Britain at the moment and the publicity given to the National Front and its policy of compulsory repatriation, there is a fear that the information on 'ethnic origin' might in future be misused. There is a fear not just about neo-fascist parties but also about the policies of the mainstream political parties. Information, rather than being used to combat the disadvantage and discrimination suffered by blacks, has not led to significant improvements in this direction. The most significant aspects of legislation have been the Immigration Acts which have successively cut black immigration and led to additional suffering – in some cases by splitting families. The progress of the legislation against racial discrimination has been slow. In areas of Housing, Education and Employment, governments have tended towards area policies to combat general disadvantage (e.g. Inner Areas), rather than policies dealing with the specific disadvantage faced by black people. In this context, the collection of information on 'ethnic origin' would seem to be superfluous.

It seems impossible to reconcile these opposing points of view. In the next section, we consider the limitations of official statistics. The problem of monitoring 'ethnic origin' is reconsidered in the conclusion and discussed in the light of this.

Problems and limitations of official statistics

The Select Committee on Race Relations and Immigration reported in March 1978: 'There are no reliable figures about immigrants now resident in the United Kingdom: no reliable statistics which can be described as indicators of immigration: and even under immigration control no official estimates published of the numbers that may be expected to be, and will be, admitted in the future in any particular category, or overall.'

It is a very difficult problem to estimate the possible future numbers of immigrants and even to obtain current estimates of immigrant numbers is not easy. The Committee underestimates these problems whilst pointing clearly to the inadequacies of the current series. The statistics on immigration come from two sources, the Home Office and the International Passenger Survey conducted by OPCS(see Chapter 1). A major problem with them is that information is collected for different purposes, which makes comparison difficult. The Home Office statistics relate to individuals subject to immigration control, patrials and non-patrials, and the IPS defines an immigrant as an individual who has lived overseas for at least one year and who intends to live in this country for at least one year. The Home Office statistics are more limited in scope but appear to be complete; the IPS statistics are wider in scope but are based on samples and are subject to sampling error.

There have been a large number of problems with the International Passenger Survey. One reason is that it is used for more than one purpose. It is funded not by OPCS but by the Department of

Industry, and its aim is to provide information on tourism and the effect of travel expenditure on the balance of payments.

The figures on immigration are therefore a by-product of this tourist monitoring process. For this reason, although the sample size is large (117,000 in 1975), most of this number are tourist passengers and the number of real immigrants is very small. In 1975 the total number of immigrants contacted by the survey was 2773. Of these 503 were immigrants arriving from the New Commonwealth, of whom only 44 were NC citizens from the West Indies and 155 from India, Bangladesh and Sri Lanka. The small sample size easily goes unnoticed in the statistics published in *Population Trends*, which give the grossed-up statistics. Thus the 503 contacts from the New Commonwealth are grossed to give an estimate of 34.9 thousand New Commonwealth immigrants arriving, and 2.9 thousand arrivals from the West Indies. The sample sizes and standard errors are published in the OPCS journal *International Migration*, which appears annually but is three years out of date when it appears (the 1975 volume appeared in 1978).[3] The percentage error $\left(100 \times \dfrac{\text{standard error}}{\text{gross estimate}}\right)$ for these figures was given for the West Indies as 18% and for India, Bangladesh and Sri Lanka as 10%. If the IPS figures were from a random sample (which they are not, so they are possibly subject to a wider margin of error), the estimate for the number of arrivals from the West Indies in 1975 is 2.9 thousand, and a 95% confidence interval is between 1.9 thousand and 3.9 thousand. This means that, to be 95% sure that the actual number of arrivals is known within a certain band, that band has to be between 1.9 and 3.9 thousand. For the purpose of reliable estimates these are unacceptable margins of error. It is important for researchers to bear in mind these limitations when using OPCS migration estimates.

Apart from the small sample size, other problems arise as a consequence of the differential sampling procedure used. The frequency with which sampling is carried out at different ports of entry is varied as it is considered to be uneconomic to maintain a 24-hour interviewing team in a port with few arrivals.

Another problem of the IPS is that some categories of traveller are omitted from the survey. The main omission is travellers to and from the Irish Republic: it is probable that some migrants enter or leave the UK via the Irish Republic. In particular, it is known that substantial numbers of passengers who are US citizens enter and leave the UK in this way.

The fact that the IPS suffers from a number of grave defects is reflected in the revisions made by OPCS to these statistics when they are not in agreement with the Home Office statistics. It was found that even allowing for the large sampling errors of the IPS and differences in definition in the categories used by the IPS and the Home Office, the IPS numbers of immigrant citizens from India, Pakistan and Bangladesh were consistently and substantially less than the Home Office numbers. The principle used for the revision was that 'the IPS estimate should not be less than the Home Office estimate for the three countries concerned'.[4] This led to the upward revision of the number of immigrants arriving from Pakistan from 6600 to 11,800 (a 78% change). Changes of this magnitude reflect a continuing doubt about the accuracy of the statistics.

An unfortunate backdrop to the current series of immigration statistics is the double counting of embarkations at Heathrow in 1973, which resulted in the net migration balance being reported as 17,000 and subsequently revised and reported in the House of Commons by Mr Roy Jenkins in November 1975 as 86,000. This 'clerical' error was seized upon by Mr Powell and claims were made that such an error could not have been a simple clerical error but that there had been a deliberate attempt to mislead the public. It is unlikely that this was the case, but the error reflects poorly on the monitoring procedures of the Home Office.

Finally, a further difficulty with both Home Office and IPS immigration statistics are the discontinuities in the series, which make changes over time difficult to monitor. The IPS Migration Statistics were published in 1964 and comparisons with statistics prior to this date are virtually impossible. Home Office statistics are difficult to monitor over time because of changes in the Immigration Law.

Estimation of the size of the black population in Britain has also been beset by statistical problems. Here again there are problems of definition and the largest technical problem has been that birthplace data has been used as an indicator of physical characteristics and 'ethnic origin'. This has led to a number of difficulties because there is not a one-to-one correspondence between the two. For example, approximately one-third of the Indian born individuals enumerated in the 1966 census were white. The difficulties arise in estimating the proportion of whites amongst children born in the UK to New Commonwealth born parents, and the proportion of whites amongst children born in the New Commonwealth to New Commonwealth born parents. In *Population Trends no. 9*[5] revisions of approximately 8% were made in a downward direction to the estimates of the New Commonwealth ethnic origin population published in *Population Trends no. 2*.[6] The estimate for mid 1974 was changed from 1.744 million to 1.615 million, i.e. the number of black people was reduced at a stroke by 129 thousand.

The main general criticism of the rest of the statistics produced by central government on the black population is that they are sparse and that they are drawn from sample surveys, in which black people are only a small proportion of the population sampled. This is an inevitable consequence of any survey which uses the total population as the sampling frame. In the General Household Survey, for example, in 1971 the sample contained 25,888 persons aged 15 or over, of whom only 482 were born in the New Commonwealth. This places severe limitations on conclusions that can be drawn, although some data can be derived by aggregating data over a number of years. The same is true of the National Dwelling and Housing Survey. The other drawback of the General Household Survey is that a distinction is made between 'coloured' and 'white' by the interviewer, a subjective categorisation which is not used by any other survey, and therefore no cross-comparisons with other surveys can be made.

Conclusion

Returning to the question of monitoring 'ethnic origin', we return to a genuine dilemma. If reliable statistical information is necessary for informed public policy decisions, then statistics on 'ethnic' minorities are needed. But on the other hand, the collection of statistics reinforces artificial social divisions and provides fuel for racist arguments. This dilemma needs to be seen in relation to the role of official statistics and their supposed objectivity.

Official statistics tend to be regarded as particularly authoritative and objective sources of data. This view is supported by the Government Statistical Service, which portrays itself as a neutral fact-finding agency, as a kind of statistical 'camera' used by the government to provide information to help run social affairs more effectively. It is a powerful analogy. Not only is it claimed that putting social facts into numerical form brings them into better focus, but there is a strong implication that any imperfections in the statistics can be treated as a purely technical problem. What is needed is to take more snaps when part of the scene has been missed out, or to develop and print the film in a different way.

This view of official statistics is, however, not the real situation at all. If taken a little further, the snapshot analogy may itself be used to challenge this view. We may go on to ask whether the nature of the numerical picture is dependent in any way upon who takes the picture, the particular instruments they use or the requirements of those who commission the picture in the first place. To pose these questions is to raise the whole issue of whose picture of society is reflected in these data. Official statistics present not a neutral picture of British society, but one developed in support of the system of power which exists in Britain – a system in which the state plays a particularly important role. The state is not neutral, neither are the statistics it collects. Social research by government and other administrators stems from a need for both monitoring and control, e.g. immigration control.[7]

This is clearly seen in the development and coverage of statistics on black people. Immigrants have fulfilled an important role in the economy in areas of mainly semi- and unskilled employment. As the economic climate changes, the economic need for immigrants and their children born here changes also. The call for immigration in the 1950s in order to staff London Transport becomes a call to stop immigration in the 1960s and 1970s. The collection of statistics reflects the need of the state to monitor these changes. Thus the statistics on population flows (immigration) and population stocks (Census statistics on New Commonwealth ethnic origin) are, for all their limitations, relatively detailed and comprehensive. The statistics on employment of ethnic minorities, on work permits and unemployment are also detailed; statistics of coloured workers registered as unemployed have been collected since 1963.

On the other hand, statistics on health, education, housing and social services are far from comprehensive. The only health statistics nationally are from national insurance records (i.e. related to employment). For research on the special health needs of black people, individual, usually small scale, research findings must be relied upon. The re-emergence of rickets in this country amongst Asians in Glasgow was noted in the early 1970s, and (until recently) there has been no national monitoring of this (and, to date, no firm initiative by central government to take action by, for example, reinforcing chapati flour with vitamin D). Other special health needs, for instance the higher incidence of tuberculosis and infant mortality amongst Asians, have been given little attention.

In education the question of monitoring 'ethnic origin' has not been resolved. The collection of statistics on immigrant children was discontinued in 1973, although there is now discussion about their reintroduction. In housing, reliance is placed on the PEP Survey by Smith and Whalley.[8] The National Dwelling and Housing Survey, 1978, commissioned by the Department of the Environment has improved the quality of statistics available, but although the survey is large (initially 375,000 households), the number of ethnic minority households is quite small. The 1971 Census provides the most comprehensive information, but is now rather dated. In social services there are no national statistics available, and very little monitoring at the local level either.[9]

In conclusion, we have widespread reservations about the uses and usefulness of existing official statistics on black people in Britain. These stem from both technical criticisms and an awareness of the political considerations that have led to the emphasis on statistics about black immigration. How, then, does one evaluate the demand that statistics on 'ethnic origin' continue to be collected in Britain? Of course, if one is committed to the eradication of racial discrimination and disadvantage, there must be some form of monitoring. However, one can be so committed but also believe that the government has no serious intention of eradicating discrimination and disadvantage. Hence, if one believes that the collection of further data is unlikely to bring about positive change (and, indeed, might even be used to the disadvantage of black people), then it is difficult to support the idea of monitoring 'ethnic origin'.

On the other hand, if one were prepared to accept government's stated commitment to the eradication of discrimination and disadvantage, one can argue that the existing statistics can be collected and produced more accurately and that their focus should shift. As we have shown, statistics on immigration are comparatively comprehensive but (in the case of the IPS) unreliable, and cross-comparisons with other statistics are difficult, if not impossible. The method of collection of these statistics could be improved and a comparison of Home Office and IPS statistics regularly published. The clear presentation of official statistics in *Population Trends* and *Social Trends* is welcomed, but these could be improved further by ensuring that sample sizes and standard errors are clearly presented, in order that users are aware of their limitations. Of course, unless one links these suggestions with a stated opposition to immigration control which is based on racist criteria, one is only asking for an improvement in the presentation of statistics which reflect those criteria. Moreover, equally important is the argument that more attention be paid to the collection of statistics about the particular circumstances and needs of black people in the areas of health, housing, education, employment and the social services.

In the final analysis, therefore, the dilemma is a political one. One's solution depends upon one's evaluation of the intentions of the state. If past history (see Chapter 2) is a useful guide to future practice, it is not easy to come to the conclusion that monitoring 'ethnic origin' in itself will have positive consequences for black people in Britain.

Notes
1. C. A. Moser, 'Statistics About Immigrants: Objectives, Sources, Methods and Problems', *Social Trends 1972*, no. 3, 1972. pp. 20–30.
2. P. Hewitt, *The Information Gatherers* (London: NCCL, 1978).
3. OPCS, *International Migration, 1975*, Series MN no. 2, London, HMSO, 1978.
4. OPCS, *International Migration, 1976*, London, HMSO, 1979, p. 8.
5. OPCS, Immigrant Statistics Unit, 'New Commonwealth and Pakistan Population Estimates', *Population Trends, 1977, no. 9.*
6. OPCS Immigrant Statistics Unit, 'Country of Birth and Colour', *Population Trends, 1976, no. 2.*
7. J. Irvine, *Demystifying Social Statistics*, Pluto Press, 1979.
8. D. Smith and A. Whalley, *Racial Minorities and Public Housing* (London: Political and Economic Planning, 1975).
9. Association of Directors of Social Services, *Multi-racial Britain: the social services response* (London: Commission for Racial Equality, 1978).

Appendix A Glossary

African Commonwealth Origin   Persons not of UK descent originating from African Commonwealth countries, including (pending the availability of more detailed census data) East African Asians.

Alien   A national of any non-Commonwealth country, including Pakistan and South Africa but excluding Ireland.

Asian   Commonly used to refer to persons born in India or Pakistan, of to descendents of such persons who were born in East Africa, who subsequently migrated to the UK. It is also used to refer to the children born in the UK of both groups. When used, it should be recognised that it refers to a wide range of persons who do not share a single, homogeneous culture but who are culturally distinct. Hence the persons to whom the term is applied do not necessarily define themselves as Asian, or if they do, do not recognise it as a predominant self-identity. The latter is less true for children born in Britain of such parents.

Black   Generally used in this book to refer to the population of New Commonwealth and Pakistani origin, that is the population born in New Commonwealth countries and Pakistan and their children born here. When used this term does not imply a cultural homogeneity among the various groups to which it refers. (This corresponds to the definition New Commonwealth and Pakistani ethnic origin used by OPCS).

Census   Population Census carried out by the Office of Population, Censuses and Surveys.

Commission for Racial Equality   Set up by 1976 Race Relations Act to promote equality of opportunity and to conduct inquiries and investigations under the Act.

Community Relations Councils Local offices in most cities responsible for community relations work under the Commission for Racial Equality.

Deportation Sending a person out of the UK under an order made by the Home Secretary.

EEC European Economic Community, of which the UK became part on 1 January 1973. Member nations are bound by the Treaty of Rome, EEC legislation and judgments of the European Court of Justice at Luxembourg. Members: France, Italy, West Germany, Holland, Belgium, Luxembourg, Denmark, Ireland, UK.

Ethnic group Used to refer to a group of persons who could identify themselves as sharing a distinct culture.

Illegal entrant This is a person who, needing permission to enter the UK (i.e. most non-patrials), fails to obtain it before entering, either because he/she bypasses immigration control altogether or because he/she obtains admission by a fundamental deception.

Illegal immigrant An illegal entrant or a person who has overstayed his leave: this term is not used in law.

Immigration Rules These are made and amended by the Home Secretary and have the force of law. They are published in four main booklets, with amendments in separate leaflets, by HM Stationery Office.

Indian sub-continent A geographical term used to refer collectively to India, Pakistan and Bangladesh.

Irish citizens The Irish are now EEC nationals. They can also enter the UK freely under the Common Travel Area provisions in the *1971 Immigration Act*, Sections 1(3) and 9.

Mediterranean Commonwealth Origin Persons not of UK descent originating from Cyprus, Gibraltar, Malta and Gozo. These persons are included in the numbers of New Commonwealth ethnic origin in OPCS statistics.

Naturalisation The process by which aliens and British Protected Persons can obtain citizenship of the UK and Colonies.

NCWP New Commonwealth and Pakistan. Used in official statistics from 1972 in order to include Pakistan, i.e. equivalent to New Commonwealth prior to 1972.

New Commonwealth The Commonwealth countries excluding the 'Old Commonwealth' – Australia, New Zealand and Canada. In

1972 Pakistan left the Commonwealth, so is included up to this date, but not afterwards.

New Commonwealth Ethnic Origin This is a term used by OPCS to refer to persons born in the New Commonwealth who are not of UK descent, plus children born in Great Britain to parents of New Commonwealth ethnic origin, including children with only one such parent.

Non-patrial A person without right of abode in the UK under the *1971 Immigration Act.*

Old Commonwealth Australia, Canada, New Zealand.

Overstayer Many non-patrials are admitted to the UK only for a limited period, and this time is stamped on the passport. A person who remains here after the date stamped on his passport and who does not apply for an extension of stay is usually described as an overstayer.

Patrial A person with the right of abode in the UK under the *1971 Immigration Act, Section 2.* Such persons must either have been born in the UK, or to have had at least one parent or grandparent born in the UK or to have lived continuously in the UK free from immigration restrictions and to have registered as a citizen of the UK and colonies.

Race (racial group) A term which was used in the late eighteenth and during the nineteenth century by scientists and public to refer to a supposedly biologically distinct section of *homo sapiens*. The scientific basis for such distinctions has now been discredited. However, the general population continues to use the terms to refer to a group of persons who they identify as having different physical features from themselves. Because this usage has no scientific validity, the term is not used as a descriptive category in this book, except where usage by others requires.

Right of abode Being free to live in, and to come and go from, the UK without being subject to immigration control: the right possessed by a patrial.

Select Committee on Race Relations and Immigration A House of Commons committee of MPs, which existed until late 1979. In December 1979, the newly established Home Affairs Committee of the House of Commons appointed a sub-committee on Race Relations and Immigration.

UKPH A term used in immigration statistics for citizens of the UK and Colonies who are non-patrial and not connected with any existing colony. Most of these are people of Indian descent, living in East Africa, India and Malaysia. Some of those in Malaysia are of Chinese descent. Small numbers of UKPHs are scattered elsewhere, e.g. Zimbabwe, Zambia and Yemen.

West Indian Commonly used to refer to persons born in the Caribbean and to persons born in the UK of such parents.

Appendix B Statistical Sources

This Appendix provides a summary list of statistical sources and references used in the main body of this book.

Statistical information available within government
The information available is summarised by government department.

1. Office of Population Censuses and Surveys (OPCS)
i. Census information   Prior to 1971, the Census contained a question on an individual's place of birth. The 1971 Census included, for the first time a question on parental birthplace and this, together with name analysis, has been used to identify the population of 'New Commonwealth and Pakistani ethnic origin' (NCWP). This is done by using the number of NCWP born as a base to which the number of children of NCWP born parents is added, including those born in Britain and the number of NCWP born who are white subtracted (e.g. the so-called White Indians whose parents were British people in India serving in the diplomatic or army services). Children of mixed marriages are included.

OPCS consider that questions on country of birth and parents' countries of birth are becoming less useful as indications of 'ethnic origin' because of the growth in the number of persons in the ethnic minorities who were born in the UK of parents themselves born in the UK.

Reference: *Census 1971, Great Britain, Country of Birth Tables,* HMSO, 1974.
Country of Birth – Supplementary Tables, HMSO, 1978.

These volumes contain information about housing, household composition, economic activity and migration, all analysed by country of birth.

ii. International Passenger Survey This survey deals with immigration and emigration. It is a sample survey carried out at seaports and airports by the Social Survey Division of OPCS, but funded by the Department of Industry. The survey was set up to give information on tourism and the effect of travel expenditure on the balance of payments, but it also gives figures on international migration.

The survey defines an immigrant as

A passenger who declares an intention to stay in the United Kingdom for an unbroken period of twelve months or more, having resided outside the United Kingdom for a year or more [and vice versa for an emigrant].

Reference: *Population Trends, HMSO.* Quarterly.
OPCS Monitors (MN series).
International Migration. Annual since 1974.

iii. Birth and Death Registration data Since 1969 the country of birth of the deceased, or of the mother and father of a newly registered child, is recorded at the time of registration in England and Wales.

Reference: *OPCS Monitors and annuals (FM1 series)* – Births.
OPCS Monitors and annuals (DH1 series) – Deaths.

2. Home Office; immigration statistics

The Home Office collect statistics of the numbers of people subject to immigration control under the *Immigration Act 1971* who are admitted into the UK. Statistics are kept in terms of country or territory issuing a passenger's passport and the basis on which they are admitted to the UK or accepted for settlement. A limited amount of information is also collected about illegal immigration into the United Kingdom.

Reference: *Control of Immigration: Statistics,* HMSO.
Annual Command paper and quarterly press Bulletin.

3. Central Statistical Office: General Household Survey (GHS)

This is a sample survey sponsored by the Central Statistical Office. As well as discovering the respondent's birthplace and also his/her parent's birthplace, the interviewer makes a subjective assessment of each person seen in the household as to whether they are 'coloured' or 'white'. The GHS is therefore one of the few sources which gives statistics based on skin colour. Fewer than 1000 black persons are included in the survey each year though some information can be gathered by adding up data over a number of years.

Reference: *General Household Survey.* HMSO, annual since 1973.

4. Department of Employment (DEm)

i. Unemployment   Statistics of black workers registered as unemployed in Great Britain have been collected since 1963. When unemployed persons register for employment those who, to the employment official, appear to be of NCWP origin, are asked in which country they were born or – if born in the United Kingdom – in which country their parents were born. Records are kept of those born (or those whose parents were born) in selected countries within certain geographical areas. Currently there are seven such areas: East Africa, other African countries, West Indies, India, Pakistan, Bangladesh, and other Commonwealth countries. Details of the number of unemployed (but not the rate of unemployment) among these groups by region in Great Britain are published quarterly in the *Department of Employment Gazette.*

ii. Labour Force Survey   In 1973, 1975, 1977 and 1979 surveys were sponsored by the EEC Statistical Office and Department of Employment and carried out by OPCS to collect labour market statistics which were comparable for the whole EEC community. The surveys covered about 90,000 households in the United Kingdom and included questions on nationality and country of birth. The 1979 survey included questions on 'ethnic origin'. The Statistical Office of the European Communities (SOEC) have published information from the 1973 and 1975 surveys in their Eurostat series of publications but this information does not include any analyses of nationality or country of birth.

iii. Work permits. The DEm also compiles information on the number of work permits issued in Great Britain to foreign national/ Commonwealth citizens: this is analysed both by industry and by the nationality of the persons to whom the permit is issued. Information is published annually in the *Department of Employment Gazette.*

Reference: *Dept. of Employment Gazette.* Quarterly.

5. Department of Education and Science (DES)

From 1966 to 1973 the DES collected statistics of the number of immigrant children attending school in England and Wales and up to 1972 published the results in their annual volume of educational statistics. Information was collected on the country of origin of children: i. born outside the British Isles to parents whose countries were abroad; and ii. born in the British Isles whose parents had lived here for less than ten years.

The Select Committee on Race Relations and Immigration which in 1972–3 looked at the subject of education, found the DES statistics unsatisfactory and on the Committee's recommendation the collection of these statistics ceased in 1973. Recently, DES have considered collecting this type of statistics again and have issued a consultative document asking for views on the reinstatement of a system for the collection of statistics on black pupils. The consultative document invites comments on who should be monitored, on whether national and/or local records should be compiled and on what basis any physical classification should be made.

Reference: Statistics of Education DES. Annual.

6. *Department of Environment (DOE)*
The DOE has commissioned a large scale survey of households in England to provide data for national and local housing policy decisions: the results became available in 1978. The *National Dwelling and Housing Survey* covers about 375,000 households (210,000 in London, 105,000 in housing stress areas and about 60,000 elsewhere), and as well as questions on occupation, tenure, amenities, employment and migration, each person was asked whether they were born in the United Kingdom and to which of a list of 'racial groups' they considered they belonged.

In addition, the DOE has issued a Consultative Paper concerning the collection by local authorities of records and information on the housing of members of 'ethnic groups'. Work has been carried out in connection with the Consultative Paper to assess the acceptability of a question on 'ethnic origin' in the context of local housing departments' activities. Some local authorities already collect information on country of birth/origin (and sometimes parents' country of birth), others such as the London Borough of Camden, Islington and Lambeth have decided to keep 'ethnic records' of applicants for council housing, applicants for transfer and in a number of other policy areas.

Reference: *National Dwelling and Household Survey*, HMSO, 1978.

7. *Department of Health and Social Security (DHSS)*
i. National Insurance records   On registering for national insurance,

immigrants are asked their date of arrival, nationality, country of birth and last address abroad. For the purpose of the DHSS statistics, 'immigrants' are people who first entered national insurance from overseas, so that young persons who were born abroad but had substantial education in this country before registering are likely to be excluded. From 1971 to 1974, DHSS examined an annual 2% sample of national insurance records, and analysed immigrants by class of insurance and country of last residence abroad. These estimates are not available for later years, but for 1975 onwards it is intended to make annual estimates for the EEC of the number of foreign workers arriving in the UK, analysed by age, sex, nationality, industry and region of residence in the UK.

ii. Medical staff (NHS and Non NHS)
The DHSS collects details of birthplace (Great Britain, Northern Ireland/Irish Republic and elsewhere) for Hospital and Community Health Medical Staff in post in England and Wales at 30 September each year; for general medical practitioners individual countries of birth are recorded for those in contract at 1 October. In addition the DHSS maintains an index which includes all registered civilian medical manpower in Great Britain whether working or not. Until recently this index related to fully and provisionally registered doctors only for whom individual country of birth is held. It now includes doctors holding temporary registration, but for most of these country of qualification is held rather than country of birth. However, this index is some years out-of-date.

iii. NHS dental staff Information on birthplace (breakdown as for medical) is only collected for those in the Hospital and Community Health Service.

iv. Other NHS staff Information is collected by DHSS on the countries of birth of student and pupil nurses and pupil midwives and on whether they were recruited before or after arrival in England.

Reference: Health and Personal Social Services, DHSS, Annual.

Overview of statistical sources
This is not an exhaustive list of references to sources but a review of some available useful sources, arranged according to the organisations from which they emanate.

1. Statistical information available within government: discussion of the statistics.

Almost all of the sources mentioned above are listed in the *Guide to Official Statistics*. Section 3.4 Migration: Race Relations gives full references to the sources listed.[1] *Social Trends 1972* contains a review article on statistics about immigrants detailing objectives, sources, methods and problems with particular reference to New Commonwealth immigrants.[2] No other general review article on the statistical sources from the government statistical service has been made public since this article.

Population Trends not only provides figures of migration flows and population estimates but also contains regular review articles on specific aspects of statistics about black people. It contains a discussion of the results of the International Passenger Survey[3] and estimates of the population of New Commonwealth 'ethnic origin'.[4] There are published discussions which summarise IPS statistics[5] and which outline the technical aspects and the limitations of the IPS.[6]

The reports of the Select Committee on Race Relations and Immigration contain discussions on and use of statistical sources. The report of session 1977/8 on Immigration[7] was particularly critical of immigration statistics whilst the report of session 1976/7 on the West Indian community[8] contains specific comments on the need for monitoring of 'ethnic origin' in schools. The position of the DES on monitoring is set out in *Education in Schools, a consultative document*.[9]

Statistics on unemployment amongst ethnic minorities are periodically contained in, and discussed, in the *Department of Employment Gazette*.[10] *Take 7 – Race Relations at Work*, published in 1972, is the report of a survey undertaken by the Department of Employment into immigrant labour relations at seven English firms.[11] In the summary of findings, statistics are given for individual firms as well as totals.

2. Local Government

Various local authorities have carried out their own demographic surveys following the cancellation of the 1976 Population Census. Some of these local authorities have included questions on 'ethnic origin' and at least one authority, Bradford, has produced population projections by 'ethnic origin'.[12]

Specific studies are occasionally carried out: for example the report

Colour and the allocation of GLC Housing by the GLC[13] was commissioned as a result of a critical study by the Runnymede Trust.[14] Another example is the report of a working party of the Association of Directors of Social Services and the Commission for Racial Equality.[15]

3. The Police
The Metropolitan Police record the number of arrests by age, type of offence and by physical characteristics. The classification of these characteristics has seven subjective categories which do not correspond with the classification used by any other organisation. These statistics appear in answer to Parliamentary questions.[16]

4. Research Bodies
Political and Economic Planning Limited (PEP) carried out a survey of the black population in 1974 which involved contact with 40,000 households.[17] The definitions used to identify numbers of ethnic minorities were based on country of origin and skin colour. The survey only identified people from Bangladesh, India, Pakistan, West Indies and African Asians (nb Black Africans were excluded).

The Runnymede Trust produces statistical reports.[18] In particular its report based on the 1% Summary Tables of the 1971 Census, *Census 1971: The Coloured Population of Great Britain*, contains basic information on the size and distribution of the coloured population of Great Britain.[19]

The Commission for Racial Equality (CRE) produces Fact Sheets on Immigration, Housing and other topics in co-operation with the Trade Unions Advisory Group. These are useful summaries of government statistics and research findings. It also published *Ethnic Minorities in Britain _ Statistical Data* which contains statistical data but no commentary.[20] *New Community*, the Journal of the CRE, includes some articles of statistical interest. In addition certain local community relations councils have produced reports on specific issues.[21]

5. Academic Research
Because information on ethnic minorities available from within government is limited it is necessary in a number of areas to rely on surveys carried out by academic researchers. Many of these are mentioned elsewhere in this book. The General Bibliography (Appendix C) lists the major surveys which have resulted in the publication of book-length reports.

6. *Other Interest Groups*

Surveys are occasionally carried out by other interest groups. As examples, Age Concern has produced a survey on elderly ethnic minorities[22] and Bethnal Green Trades Council has produced a survey on racial violence in the East End of London.[23]

Notes

1. Central Statistical Office, *Guide to Official Statistics no. 1* (London: HMSO, 1976).
2. C. A. Moser, 'Statistics about immigrants: objectives, sources, methods and problems', *Social Trends,* 1972, 3.
3. N. Davies and C. Walker, 'Migrants entering and leaving the UK, 1964–74', *Population Trends,* 1975, no. 1; C. Walker, 'Demographical characteristics of migrants', *Population Trends,* 1971, no. 8.
4. Office of Population and Census Study (OPCS), Immigrant Statistics Unit, 'Country of birth and colour', *Population Trends, 1976, no. 2; OPCS Immigrant Statistics Unit, 'New Commonwealth and Pakistan population estimates', Population Trends,* 1977, no. 9; OPCS Immigrant Statistics Unit, 'Marriage and birth patterns among the New Commonwealth and Pakistan population', *Population Trends,* 1978, no. 11.
5. OPCS Demographical Review 1977, *Series DR, no. 1* (London: HMSO, 1978).
6. OPCS *International Migration 1975,* Series MN, no. 2 (London: HMSO, 1978).
7. Select Committee on Race Relations and Immigration, *Immigration* (London: HMSO, 1978).
8. Select Committee on Race Relations and Immigration, *The West Indian Community* (London: HMSO, 1977).
9. Department of Education and Science, *Education in Schools* (London: HMSO, 1977).
10. Department of Employment, 'Unemployment among workers from racial minority groups', *Department of Employment Gazette,* September 1975.
11. Department of Employment *'Take 7 – Race Relations at Work';* London: HMSO, 1972.
12. City of Bradford Metropolitan Council, *District Trends,* Bradford, 1979.
13. J. Parker et al., *Colour and the Allocation of GLC Housing* (London: GLC Research Report no. 21, 1976).
14. Runnymede Trust, *Race and Council Housing in London,* London, 1975.
15. Association of Directors of Social Services and Commission for Racial Equality *Multi-Racial Britain: The Social Services Response* (London: CRE, 1978).
16. *House of Commons Hansard;* Written Answers in Issue no. 1166, cols. 205–10, 13 December 1978.
17. D. Smith, *The Facts of Racial Disadvantage* (London: PEP, 1976). See also D. Smith, *Racial Disadvantage in Britain* (Harmondsworth: Penguin, 1977).
18. C. Demuth, *Immigration: A brief guide to the numbers game* (London: Runnymede Trust, 1978).
19. G. Lomas, *Census 1971: The Coloured Population of Great Britain* (London: Runnymede Trust, 1973).
20. Commission for Racial Equality, *Ethnic Minorities in Britain – Statistical Data* (London: CRE, 1976).
21. For example, Wandsworth Council for Community Relations, *Asians and the Health Service,* London, 1978. Redbridge Council for Community Relations, *Cause for Concern: West Indian Pupils in Redbridge,* London, 1978.
22. Age Concern, *Elderly Ethnic Minorities,* London, 1974.
23. Bethnal Green and Stepney Trades Council, *Blood on the Streets,* London, 1978.

Appendix C
General Bibliography

This is a list of books about black people in Britain. The list is not exhaustive but aims to include books which either deal in greater depth with the issues and information dealt with in this text or discuss matters not raised here. Some books were written primarily for an academic audience but all should be of interest and intelligible to the 'general reader'. A much more detailed bibliography is published by the Runnymede Trust. The latter also includes references to articles in relevant journals: *Race and Class, Race Today, New Community* and *Ethnic and Racial Studies*. Readers searching for more detailed discussions of selected topics should consult back issues of these journals.

Bagley, C., *A Comparative Perspective on the Education of Black Children in Britain,* Centre for Information and Advice on Educational Disadvantage, 1977.

Barrett Brown, M., *The Economics of Imperialism* (Harmondsworth: Penguin, 1975).

Banton, M., *The Idea of Race* (London: Tavistock, 1977).

Billig, M., *Fascists* (London: Harcourt Brace Jovanovich, 1978).

Bohning, W. R., *The Migration of Workers in the United Kingdom and the European Community* (London: Oxford University Press, 1972).

Bolt, C., *Victorian Attitudes to Race* (London: Routledge and Kegan Paul, 1971).

Brooks, D., *Race and Labour in London Transport* (London: Oxford University Press, 1975).

Cashmore, E., *Rastaman* (London: Allen and Unwin, 1979).

Castles, S. and Kosack, G., *Immigrant Workers and Class Structure in Western Europe* (London: Oxford University Press, 1973).

Coard, B., *How the West Indian Child is Made Educationally Sub-Normal in the British School System* (London: New Beacon Books, 1971).

Deakin, N., *Colour, Citizenship and British Society* (London: Panther, 1970).

Desai, R., *Indian Immigrants in Britain* (London: Oxford University Press, 1963).

Dixon, R., *Catching Them Young. Sexist, Racist and Class Images in Children's Books* (London: Pluto Press, 1977).

Dummett, A., *A Portrait of English Racism* (Harmondsworth: Penguin, 1973).

Edwards, V., *The West Indian Language Issue in British Schools* (London: Routledge and Kegan Paul, 1979).

Foner, N., *Jamaica Farewell* (London: Routledge and Kegan Paul, 1979).

Foot, P., *Immigration and Race in British Politics* (Harmondsworth: Penguin, 1966).

Gerrard, J. A., *The English and Immigration: A Comparative Study of the Jewish Influx, 1880–1910* (London: Oxford University Press, 1971).

Giles, R., *The West Indian Experience in British Schools* (London: Heinemann, 1977).

Hall, S. et al., *Policing the Crisis: Mugging, the State and Law and Order* (London: Macmillan, 1978).

Hartmann, P. and Husband, C. *Racism and the Mass Media* (London: Davis–Poynter, 1974).

Hiro, D., *Black British, White British* (Hardmondsworth: Penguin, 1971).

Humphry, D., *Police Power and Black People* (London: Panther, 1972).

Humphry, D. and Ward, M., *Passports and Politics* (Harmondsworth: Penguin, 1974).

Husband, C. (ed.), *White Media and Black Britain* (London: Arrow, 1975).

Jackson, J. A., *The Irish in Britain* (London: Routledge and Kegan Paul, 1963).

James, A. G. *Sikh Children in Britain* (London: Oxford University Press, 1974).

Jeffrey, P., *Migrants and Refugees: Muslim and Christian Pakistani Families in Bristol* (London: Cambridge University Press, 1976).

Jones, C., *Immigration and Social Policy in Britain* (London: Tavistock, 1977).

Jones, K. and Smith, A. D., *The Economic Impact of Commonwealth Immigration* (London: Cambridge University Press, 1970).

Kamin, L. J., *The Science and Politics of IQ* (Harmondsworth: Penguin, 1978).

Katznelson, I., *Black Men, White Cities* (London: Oxford University Press, 1973).

Lambert, J., *Crime, Police and Race Relations* (London: Oxford University Press, 1970).

Lawrence, D., *Black Migrants, White Natives: A Study of Race Relations in Nottingham* (London: Cambridge University Press, 1974).

Lee, T. R., *Race and Residence: The Concentration and Dispersal of Immigrants in London* (London: Oxford University Press, 1977).

Lester, A. and Bindman, G., *Race and Law* (Harmondsworth: Penguin, 1972).

Macdonald, I., *Race Relations: The New Law* (London: Butterworths, 1977).

Miles, R. and Phizacklea, A. (eds.), *Racism and Political Action in Britain* (London: Routledge and Kegan Paul, 1979).

Milner, D., *Children and Race* (Harmondsworth: Penguin, 1975).

Moore, R., *Racism and Black Resistance in Britain* (London: Pluto Press, 1975).

Moore, R. and Wallace, T., *Slamming the Door: The Administration of Immigration Control* (London: Martin Robertson, 1975).

Nugent, N. and King, R., *The British Right* (Farnborough: Saxon House, 1977).

Patterson, S., *Immigration and Race Relations in Britain 1960–1968* (London: Oxford University Press, 1969).

Peach, C. *West Indian Migration to Britain* (London: Oxford University Press, 1968).

Phizacklea, A. and Miles, R., *Labour and Racism* (London: Routledge and Kegan Paul, 1981).

Pryce, K., *Endless Pressure* (Harmondsworth: Penguin, 1979).

Rex, J. and Moore, R., *Race, Community and Conflict* (London: Oxford University Press, 1967).

Rex, J., *Race, Colonisation and The City* (London: Routledge and Kegan Paul, 1975).

Rex, J. and Tomlinson, S., *Colonial Immigrants in a British City* (London: Routledge and Kegan Paul, 1979).

Richardson, K. and Spears, D. (eds.), *Race, Culture and Intelligence* (Harmondsworth: Penguin, 1972).

Rose, E. J. B. et al., *Colour and Citizenship: A Report on British Race Relations* (London: Oxford University Press, 1969).

Saifullah Khan, V. (ed.), *Minority Families in Britain: Support and Stress* (London: Macmillan, 1979).

Smith, D. J., *Racial Disadvantage in Britain* (Harmondsworth: Penguin, 1977).

Taylor, J. H., *The Half-Way Generation: A study of Asian Youths in Newcastle-upon-Tyne* (London: National Foundation for Education and Research, 1976).

Tinker, H. *The Banyon Tree* (London: Oxford University Press, 1977).

Townsend, H. E. R. and Brittan, E., *Organisation in Multi-Racial Schools* (London: National Foundation for Education and Research, 1972).

Twaddle, M. (ed.), *Expulsion of a Minority: Essays on Ugandan Asians* (London: Athlone Press, 1975).

Walker, M., *The National Front* (London: Fontana, 1977).

Wallman, S. (ed.), *Ethnicity at Work* (London: Macmillan, 1979).

Watson, J. L., *Between Two Cultures: Migrants and Minorities in Britain* (Oxford: Blackwell, 1977).

Williams, E., *Capitalism and Slavery* (London: Deutsch, 1944).

Wilson, A., *Finding A Voice* (London: Virago, 1978).

Zubaida, S., (ed.), *Race and Racialism* (London: Tavistock, 1970).

Appendix D Runnymede Trust Publications

This contains a list of pamphlets and short books published by the Runnymede Trust on particular topics. They can be obtained directly from the Runnymede Trust at 62 Chandos Place, London WC2N 4HG (01-836 3266).

Reports
1970
Bosanquet, Nicholas, Commonwealth Immigration: The Economic Effects, 25p + p&p 15p.

Thakur, M., Industry as Seen by Immigrant Workers, 15p + p&p 10p.

Harrison, R. M., Union Policy and Workplace Practice, 15p + p&p 10p.

Allen, Sheila and Bornat, Joanna, Unions and Immigrant Workers: How they See Each Other, 15p + p&p 10p.

1971
Mbayah, M., Harrison, R. and the Runnymede Trust Industrial Unit, A Race Relations Audit, £1 + p&p 25p.

Rees, T., Policy or Drift?, 15p + p&p 10p.

Adeney, Martin, Community Action – Four Examples, 25p + p&p 15p.

Bohning, W. R. and Stephen, D., The EEC and the Migration of Workers, 25p + p&p 15p.

The Trade Union Movement and Discrimination, Essays by Jack Jones, Tony Corfield, Shella Allen and Lord Delacourt-Smith, 25p + p&p 15p.

1972

Sand, J. and McDonald, L. D., The Invisible Immigrants, 50p + p&p 15p.

Eversley, David, A Question of Numbers, 35p + p&p 15p.

John, Augustine, Race in the Inner City, 25p + p&p 15p.

Hayes, M., Community Relations and the Role of the Community Relations Commission in Northern Ireland, 10p + p&p 10p.

Lester, Anthony, Citizens Without Status, 10p + p&p 10p.

Burney, E. and Wainwright, D., After Four Years, 15p + p&p 10p.

1973

Pahl, R. E., London What Next?, 50p + p&p 15p.

Pulle, Stanislaus, Police/Immigrant Relations in Ealing, 50p + p&p 15p.

Stewart, Margaret, A Stitch in Time, 25p + p&p 15p.

Lomas, Gillian B., Census 1971: The Coloured Population of Great Britain, £1.00 + p&p 30p.

1974

Pollak, L. H., Discrimination in Employment: The American Response, 65p + p&p 15p.

Akram, M., Where Do You Keep Your String Beds?, 50p + p&p 15p.

Trade Unions and Immigrant Workers, Joint WEA and Runnymede Trust publication, 18p (postage included).

1975

Jupp, Tom and Davies, Evelyn, The Background and Employment of Asian Immigrants, £4 + p&p 60p.

Bindman, G. and Rendel, M., The Sex Discrimination Bill, Race and the Law, 65p + p&p 15p.

Stephen, David, Minority Rights and Minority Morale in the USA – How relevant is US Experience?, 25p + p&p 15p.

Barker, Anthony, Strategy and Style in Local Community Relations, £1 + p&p 20p.

Brooks, Dennis, Black Employment in the Black Country: A Study of Walsall, 90p + p&p 20p.

Shah, Samir, Immigrants and Employment in the Clothing Industry, The Rag Trade in London's East End, £1.30 + p&p 20p.

Racial Discrimination: A Guide to the Government's White Paper, 60p + p&p 15p.

Lomas, Gillian and Monck, E. M., Census 1971 – The Coloured Population of Great Britain: A Comparative Study of Coloured Households in Four County Boroughs, £2.00 + p&p 30p.

1976

Pope, David, Community Relations – The Police Response, £1.50 + p&p 20p.

Race Relations at Work: An Education and Action Programme, Free p&p 10p.

Dummett, Ann, Citizenship and Nationality, £1.50 + p&p 20p.

Evans, Peter, Published and be Damned?, £1.30 + p&p 15p.

Gujerati Welfare Rights Handbook, 25p + p&p 15p.

1977

Khan, Shamim, and Pearn, M. A., Worktalk Manual, £3 + p&p 30p.

Akram, M. and Elliot, J., Appeal Dismissed, £2 + p&p 55p.

Dummett, Ann, British Nationality Law – A Guide to the Green Paper, 50p + p&p 10p.

1978

Demuth, Clare, 'Sus' – A report on the Vagrancy Act 1824, £1.50 + p&p 15p.

Dummett, Ann, A New Immigration Policy, £2 + p&p 15p.

Pearn, M. A., Employment Testing and the Goal of Equal Opportunity: The American Experience, £1.25 + p&p 25p.

Horabin, Roshan, Problems of Asians in Penal Institutions, 75p + p&p 15p.

Pearn, M. A., Increasing Employability: An Evaluation of the Full-employ Training Scheme, Free + p&p 20p.

1979

A Review of the Race Relations Act 1976: proceedings of a one day seminar organised by the Runnymede Trust, £2 + p&p 40p.

1980

Discriminating Fairly: A Guide to Fair Selection. A Report by the Runnymede Trust/British Psychological Society Joint Working Party on Employment and Racial Discrimination, £2 + p&p 20p.

Briefing papers

1975

Review of Race Relations Legislation, Runnymede Trust, 20p + p&p 10p.

1976

Race Relations Bill, Runnymede Trust, 20p + p&p 15p.

Race Relations Bill Briefing Group Briefs, Runnymede Trust, set of 10 at £1.00 + p&p 35p per set.

The Runnymede Trust's Submission to the Parliamentary Select Committee on Race Relations and Immigration – West Indians in Britain, Runnymede Trust, free + p&p 10p.

1977

Smith, D. J., The Facts of Racial Disadvantage – A Summary, 20p + p&p 10p.

Commission for Racial Equality, 'Discussion about the role of the CRE', Runnymede Trust, 20p + p&p 10p.

Khan, Verity Saifullah, Bilingualism and Linguistic Minorities in Britain – Developments, Perspectives, 20p + p&p 12p.

The Role of Immigrants in the Labour Market – A summary, Runnymede Trust, Free + p&p 15p.

Akram, M. and Elliot, J., Appeal Dismissed – A Summary, 20p + p&p 10p.

Dummett, Ann, British Nationality and the Colonies, 20p + p&p 10p.

1978

A Schizoid Report, Runnymede Trust, 20p + p&p 12p.

Saunders, Cheryl, Census 1981 – Question on Racial and Ethnic Origin, 30p + p&p 12p.

Demuth, Clare, Immigration – a brief guide to the numbers game, 20p + p&p 12p.

Pearn, M. A., Beyond Tokenism – Equal employment opportunities policies, 30p + p&p 12p.

Campbell-Platt, Kiran, revised by Nicholas, Shān, Linguistic Minorities in Britain, 20p + p&p 12p.

1979

Pearn, M. A., Monitoring Equal Opportunity in the Civil Service: A Review of a Report by the Tavistock Institute, 30p + p&p 10p.

Seear, Rt Hon Baroness, The Management of Equal Opportunity, 40p + p&p 15p.

A Guide to the Government's White Paper 'Proposals for revision of the Immigration Rules', Runnymede Trust, 75p + p&p 20p.

Census 1981: The Race Question, Proceedings of a One-Day Seminar, Runnymede Trust/Cobden Trust, £1.20 + p&p 15p.

Language Testing and Indirect Discrimination: Lessons of the British Steel Case, 75p + p&p 25p.

1980

Dummett, Ann, Nationality Law, £1.20 + p&p 15p.

Russell, Ralph, Ethnic Minority Languages and the Schools (with special reference to Urdu), £1.20 + p&p 15p.

Lewis, Robin, Real Trouble, £1.25 + p&p 25p.

Nicol, A. G. L., Public Order Act 1936 and related legislation, £1.50 + p&p 25p.

Inner Cities and Black Minorities, Runnymede Trust, N.C.V.O., £1.50 + p&p 25p.

Appendix E Commission for Racial Equality Publications

This contains a selection of short books and pamphlets published by the Commission for Racial Equality. They can be obtained by writing to the Commission for Racial Equality at Elliot House, 10–12 Allington Street, London SW1E 5EH (01-828 7022).

Educational Needs of Children from Minority Groups (50p)

The Education of Ethnic Minority Children (80p)

In-service Education of Teachers in Multi-racial Areas: An evaluation of current practice (60p)

Meeting Their Needs: An account of language tuition schemes for ethnic minority women (80)

The employment of Non-English Speaking Workers: What industry must do (50p)

World Religions: a handbook for teachers (£1.50)

Housing in Multi-racial Areas: A report of a working party of Housing Directors (60p)

Housing Choice and Ethnic Concentration: An attitude study (90p)

Ethnic Minorities in the Inner City: The ethnic dimension in urban deprivation in England (by C. Cross) (£1.80)

Unemployment and Homelessness: A report (£1)

Urban Deprivation, Racial Inequality and Social Policy: A report (£1.75)

Fostering Black Children (30p)

Multi-racial Britain: Social services response (£1)

Who Minds? A study of working mothers and childminding in ethnic minority communities (75p)

Participation of Ethnic Minorities in the General Election, October 1974 (45p)

Between Two Cultures: a study in relationships between generations in the Asian community in Britain (by M. Anwar) (£1)

Appendix F Institute of Race Relations Publications

This contains a list of pamphlets published by the Institute of Race Relations, 247 Pentonville Road, London N1 9NG. (01-837 0041).

Sivanandan, A., Race, Class and the State: the black experience in Britain; Race and Class Pamphlet no. 1, 30p.

Edgar, David, Fascism and the Politics of the National Front; Race and Class Pamphlet no. 4, 30p.

Sivanandan, A., From Immigration Controls to 'Induced Repatriation'; Race and Class Pamphlet no. 5, 20p.

Institute of Race Relations, Police Against Black People – Evidence submitted to the Royal Commission on Criminal Procedure; Race and Class Pamphlet no. 6, 95p.

Appendix G SSRC Research Unit on Ethnic Relations Publications

This is a list of Working Papers published by the SSRC Research Unit on Ethnic Relations at University of Aston, St. Peter's College, College Road, Saltley, Birmingham B8 3TE (021-327-0194).

No. 1 Fenton, Mike and Collard, David, Do Coloured Tenants Pay More? Some Evidence, 56p.

No. 2 Fenton, Mike, Asian Households in Owner-Occupation – a Study of the Pattern, Costs and Experiences of Households in Greater Manchester, 77p.

No. 3 Brah, A., Fuller, M., Louden, D. and Miles, R., Experimenter Effects and the Ethnic Cueing Phenomenon, 56p.

No. 4 Flett, H. and Peaford, M., The Effect of Slum Clearance on Multi-occupation, 71p.

No. 5 Flett, H., Council Housing and the Location of Ethnic Minorities, 71p.

No. 6 Miles, R. and Phizacklea, A., The TUC, Black Workers, and New Commonwealth Immigration, 1954–1973, 66p.

No. 7 Clark, David, Immigrant Responses to the British Housing Market: A Case Study in the West Midlands Conurbation, 84p.

No. 8 Banton, Michael, Rational Choice: a Theory of Racial and Ethnic Relations, £1.25.

No. 9 Leach, Bridget, Youth and Spatial Poverty: Activity Space Patterns of Black and White Young People in Leeds, £1.70.

No. 10 Miles, Robert, Between Two Cultures? The Case of Rastafarianism, £1.25.

No. 11 Elliott, Margaret, Shifting Patterns in Multi-occupation, £1.40.

No. 12 Flett, Hazel, Black Council House Tenants in Birmingham, £1.95.

Index